origami
fun and games

marc kirschenbaum

fit to print publishing, inc.
new york, ny

Origami Fun and Games
Copyright © 2020
Fit To Print Publishing, Inc.

ISBN 978-1-951146-13-9 (Paperback Edition)
ISBN 978-1-951146-14-6 (Hardcover Edition)

The diagrams in this book were produced with Macromedia's Freehand, and image processing was done with Adobe Photoshop. The Backtalk family of typefaces was used for the body text and the cover and headers use Helvetica. Ellen Cohen assisted with the cover design and provided valuable artistic assistance.

Contents

Introduction   5
Symbols and Terminology   6
Sailboat   10
Matryoshka Doll   14
Fortune Cookie   18
Tent   20
Pencil   22
Puddle Jumper   25
Tennis Racket   29
Baker   33
Building Block   38
Television   40
Camera   44
Electric Guitar   49
Matchbox   53
Skier   60
Golfer   69
Top   77
Fluffy (Teddy Bear)   81
Jack-in-the-box   91
Chess Pieces   104
Chessboard   119

Introduction

For many people origami is the perfect pastime. It fuels both analytical and creative juices with the convenience of readily available papers. Even the most fanatical paper folding hobbyists have other interests to keep themselves busy and this collection celebrates these diversions through origami, of course!

Being physically active is important and pieces like the *Tennis Racket* and *Skier* commemorate some of the more demanding sports. Models like the *Golfer*, *Tent* and *Sailboat* acknowledge those who prefer a slower pace. A paper *Television* is included for those who consider getting up from a couch as an exercise. Having other creative outlets is appreciated through models like the *Baker*, *Camera* and *Electric Guitar*.

Kids along with more playful adults like toys, and this compilation depicts a few of them. A classically styled *Jack-in-the-box* is included and there are two types of dolls represented. *Fluffy* portrays a typical Western teddy bear and the *Matryoshka Doll* mimics the stacking capability of this traditional doll. Models like the *Building Block* and *Pencil* reflect more cerebral pastimes. The *Top* really spins, and the *Puddle Jumper* will stay aloft just like the toy it is based on. The *Matchbox* is another model that has an action element with its working tray. You can fill the *Fortune Cookie* with serious proverbs or fun fantasies.

Many pages are devoted towards the popular game of chess. The *Chessboard* weaves the outer edges of the square to produce the checkered pattern. Large paper will be needed for this one, as the resulting board is only $1/5^{th}$ the height of the starting square. The *Chess Pieces* were engineered to all start with the same sized square and are closely related, sharing the same standing base.

All these pieces follow the one square no cuts philosophy. This makes for some interesting and sometimes challenging folding sequences. These origami models are arranged by their approximate level of difficulty, so you can work your way up to the harder ones. Enjoy!

Symbols and Terminology

Line Styles

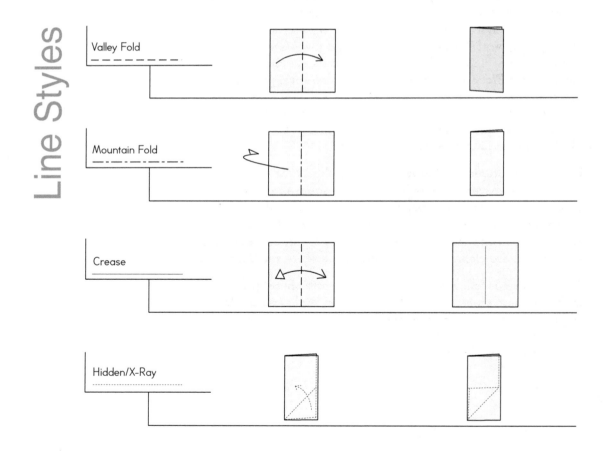

Valley Fold

Mountain Fold

Crease

Hidden/X-Ray

Arrows

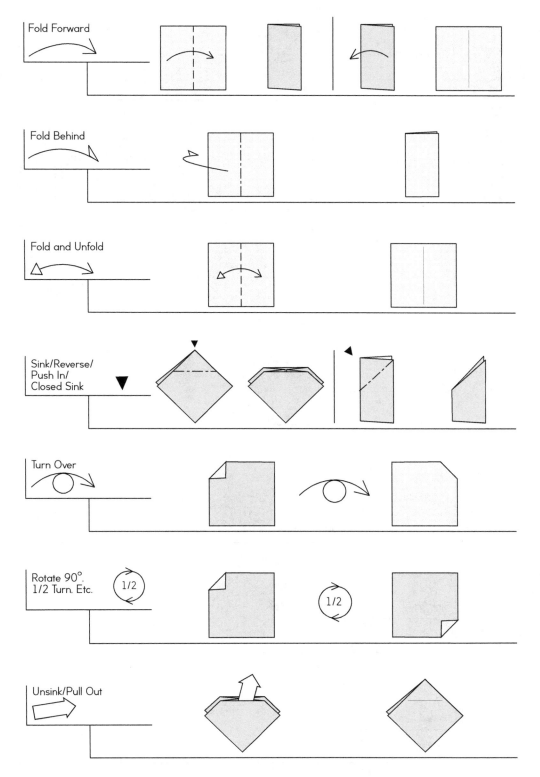

Fold Forward

Fold Behind

Fold and Unfold

Sink/Reverse/
Push In/
Closed Sink

Turn Over

Rotate 90°.
1/2 Turn. Etc.

1/2

Unsink/Pull Out

Maneuvers

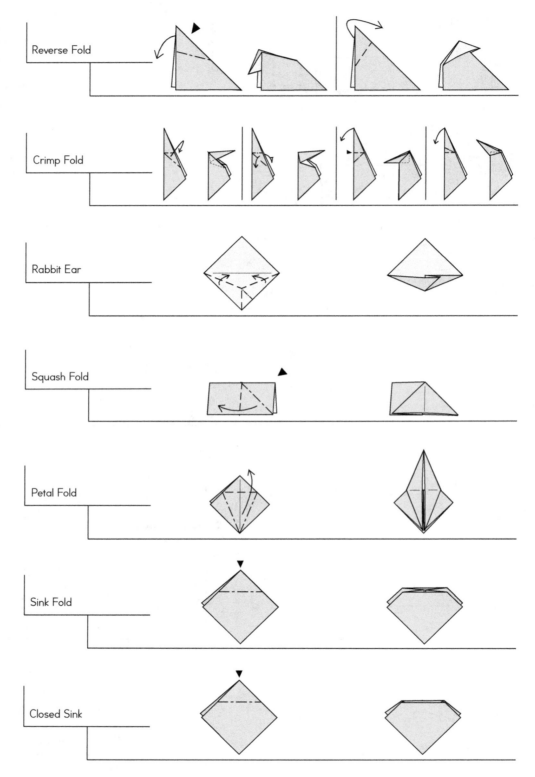

Reverse Fold

Crimp Fold

Rabbit Ear

Squash Fold

Petal Fold

Sink Fold

Closed Sink

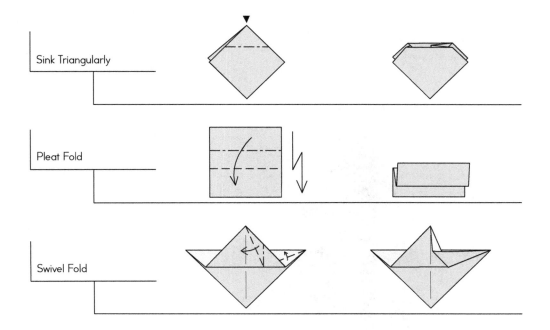

Sink Triangularly

Pleat Fold

Swivel Fold

Sailboat

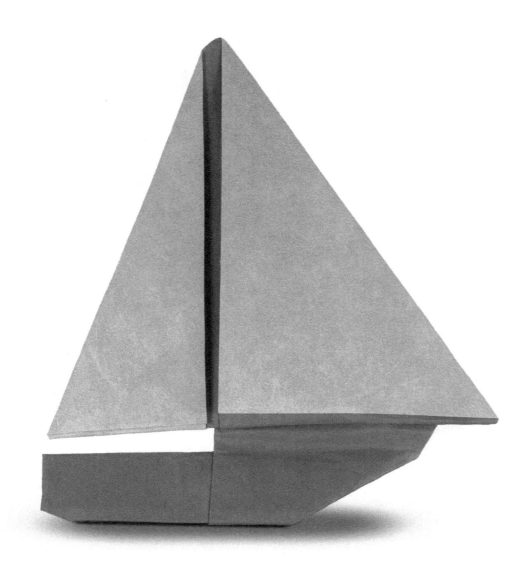

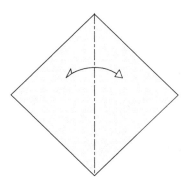

1. Precrease the diagonal with a mountain fold.

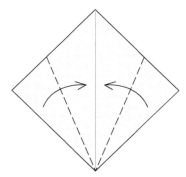

2. Valley fold the sides to the center.

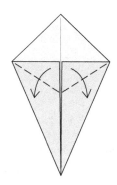

3. Valley fold the edges outwards.

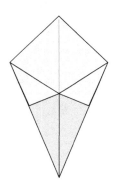

4. Turn over.

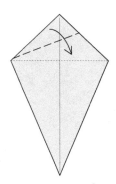

5. Valley fold towards the imaginary edge, leaving a small gap from the corner.

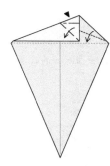

6. Squash fold the other side down to match.

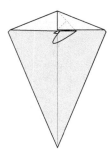

7. Mountain fold the hidden corner inside.

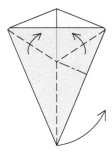

8. Rabbit ear the flap over.

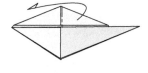

9. Swing the rear flap to the other side.

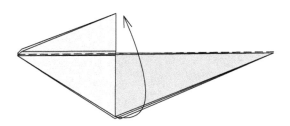

10. Open out the top layer.

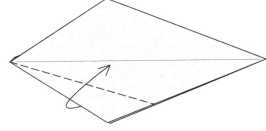

11. Valley fold to the center.

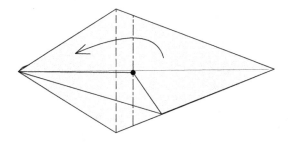

12. Pleat the flap, noting the dotted intersection.

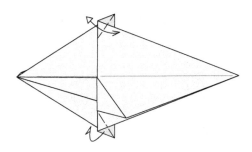

13. Precrease at the top and mountain fold at the bottom.

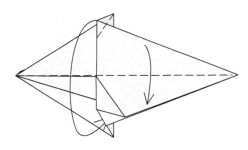

14. Valley fold in half, tucking the flap into the pocket.

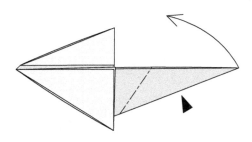

15. Reverse fold, leaving a small gap at the middle.

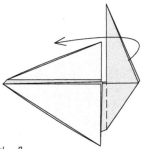

16. Open out the flap.

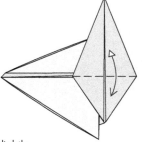

17. Precrease lightly.

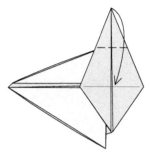

18. Valley fold to the last crease.

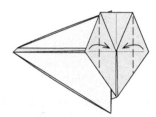

19. Valley fold the sides, leaving a small gap at the center.

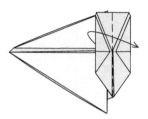

20. Valley fold in half.

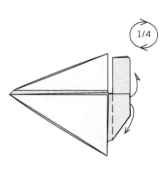

21. Rotate the model and open out the bottom slightly so the model will stand.

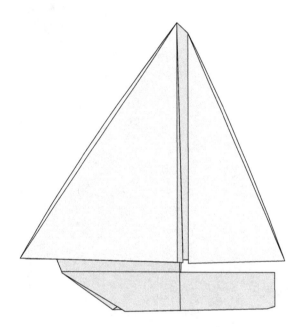

22. Completed *Sailboat*.

Matryoshka

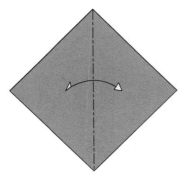

1. Precrease the diagonal with a mountain fold.

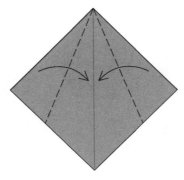

2. Valley fold the sides to the center.

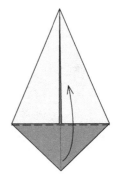

3. Valley fold the corner up.

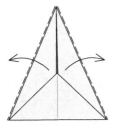

4. Open out the side flaps.

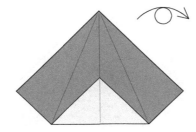

5. Turn over.

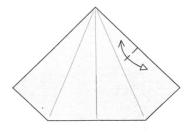

6. Pinch the edge in half.

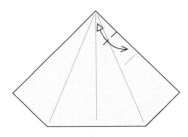

7. Pinch the upper section in half.

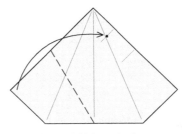

8. Starting the fold from the bottom center, valley fold the corner to the crease.

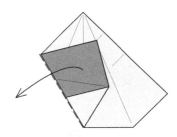

9. Unfold the flap.

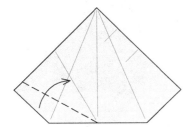

10. Valley fold to the crease.

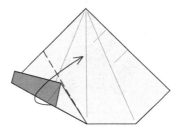

11. Valley fold along the existing crease.

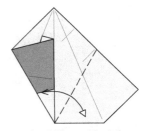

12. Precrease by folding to the left edge and unfolding.

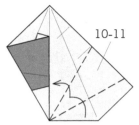

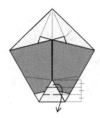

13. Repeat steps 10-11 on the right side.

14. Valley fold to the dotted intersection of creases.

15. Pleat the flap into thirds. This will be the stand for the model.

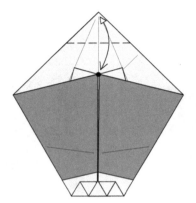

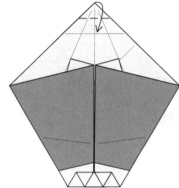

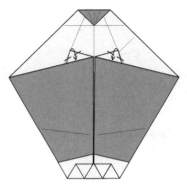

16. Precrease towards the dotted intersection.

17. Valley fold to the last crease.

18. Valley fold the corners to the edges.

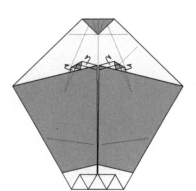

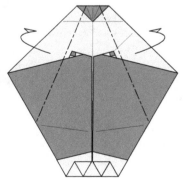

19. Mountain fold the sides of each flap.

20. Mountain fold along the existing creases.

21. Precrease the top flap.

22. Valley fold to the last crease.

23. Valley fold along the existing crease.

24. Mountain fold behind.

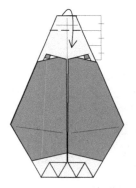

25. Valley fold in at about 1/3rd the height of the lighter section.

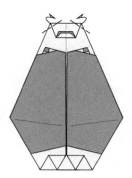

26. Mountain fold the corners.

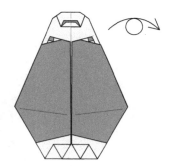

27. Turn over.

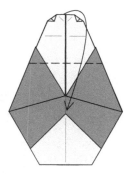

28. Valley fold towards the tip of the flap.

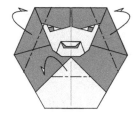

29. Mountain fold the sides and the tip of the flap. Pull out the stand from behind. You can stack smaller Matryoshkas on this stand.

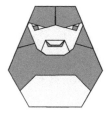

30. Completed *Matryoshka Doll*.

Fortune Cookie

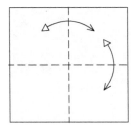

1. Precrease the sides in half.

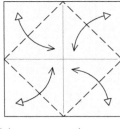

2. Fold the corners to the center and unfold.

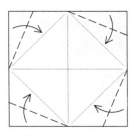

3. Valley fold towards the creases.

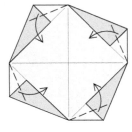

4. Valley fold the other edges along the angle bisectors.

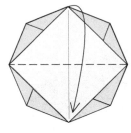

5. Valley fold in half.

6. Valley fold in half.

7. Valley fold so the corners meet.

8. Squash fold the flap.

9. Precrease the sides.

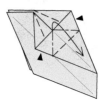

10. Petal fold the flap.

11. Mountain fold behind.

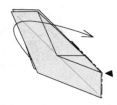

12. Pull the top layers over to the other side while inverting the corner.

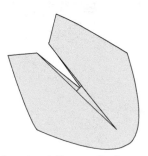

13. Completed *Fortune Cookie*.

Tent

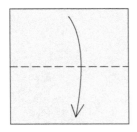

1. Valley fold in half.

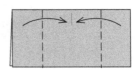

2. Pinch the top edge in half.

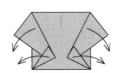

3. Valley fold the sides to the center.

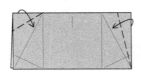

4. Valley fold the sides outwards.

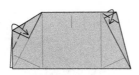

5. Valley fold the corners up.

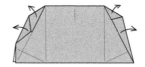

6. Unfold the sides.

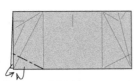

7. Valley fold along the indicated angle bisectors.

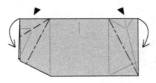

8. Valley fold the corners in as indicated.

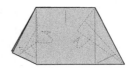

9. Unfold the sides.

10. Mountain fold the corners in along the existing creases.

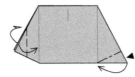

11. Reverse fold at the right side and crimp at the left side.

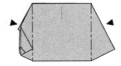

12. Fold the hidden flaps along their existing creases.

13. Fold the hidden flap along the existing crease.

14. Reverse fold at the right side and valley fold the corners at the left side.

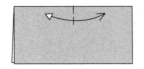

15. Push the sides in, making the model three-dimensional.

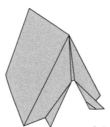

16. Completed *Tent*.

Pencil

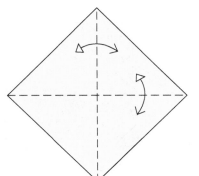

1. Precrease along the diagonals.

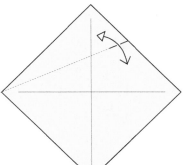

2. Pinch the edge along the angle bisector.

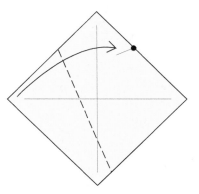

3. Valley fold the corner to the dotted crease.

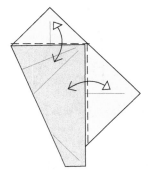

4. Precrease along the raw edges.

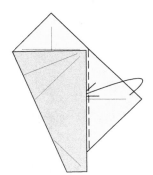

5. Tuck the side flap under.

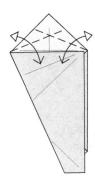

6. Precrease along the angle bisectors.

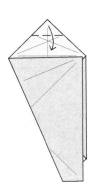

7. Valley fold down starting where the creases hit the edges. Turn over.

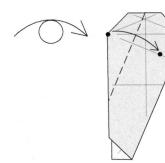

8. Valley fold the dotted corner so it hits the dotted crease.

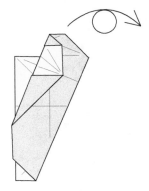

9. Turn over.

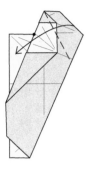
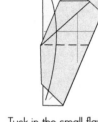

10. Mountain fold the corner. Turn over.

11. Valley fold so the edge hits the dotted intersection of edges.

12. Squash fold.

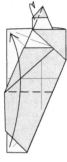
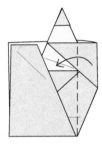

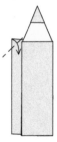

13. Tuck in the small flap at the top with a mountain fold. Valley fold the bottom edge upwards.

14. Valley fold the edge.

15. Valley fold the corner.

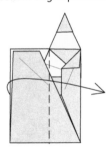
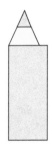

16. Valley fold the flap over.

17. Turn over.

18. Valley fold the corner.

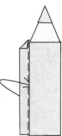
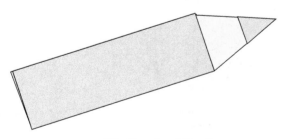

19. Tuck the flap in to lock the model.

20. Completed *Pencil*.

Puddle Jumper

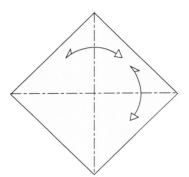

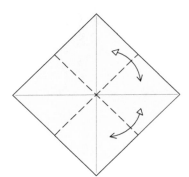

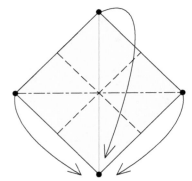

1. Precrease the diagonals with mountain folds.

2. Precrease the sides in half.

3. Bring the three corners to the bottom corner and collapse flat.

4. Reverse fold the sides.

5. Reverse fold the rear flaps.

6. Swing the front and back flaps up.

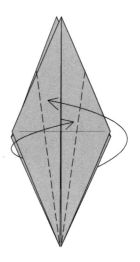

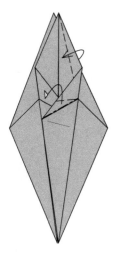

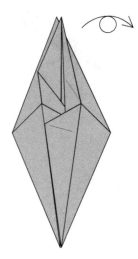

7. Valley fold the sides so they overlap.

8. Swivel fold the edge inside.

9. Turn over.

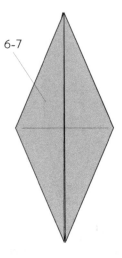

6-7

10. Repeat steps 6-7.

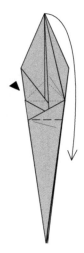

11. Pull the top flap down, allowing the center to squash flat.

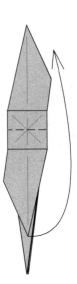

12. Swing the flap back up.

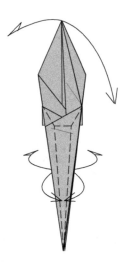

13. Valley fold the sides to the center at each side while opening out the top flaps. The folds will curve at the top and not completely flatten.

14. View the model from above.

15. Loosely pleat the sides at the suggested approximate angle. This will determine the lift when flying.

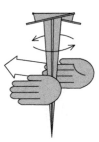

16. View from previous step. To fly, quickly spin the flap along the palm of one hand.

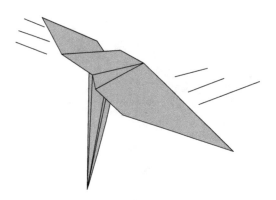

17. Completed *Puddle Jumper*.

Tennis Racket

1. Valley fold in half.

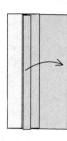

2. Valley fold the top layer in half.

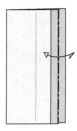

3. Valley fold to the edge.

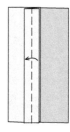

4. Valley fold to the edge.

5. Unfold the pleat, leaving the last fold in place.

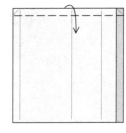

6. Precrease the back layer with a mountain fold.

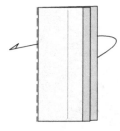

7. Open out along the center.

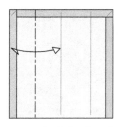

8. Precrease the top corners.

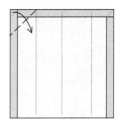

9. Valley fold the top edge down to align with the last creases.

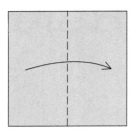

10. Valley fold the side edge in along the existing crease.

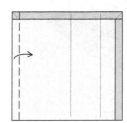

11. Precrease the left side in half.

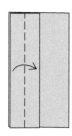

12. Valley fold towards the last crease.

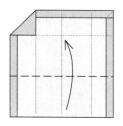

13. Valley up to meet the edge of the triangular flap.

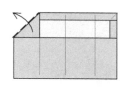

14. Open out the flap.

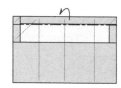

15. Mountain fold the colored edge behind.

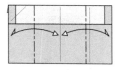

16. Precrease the sides in half with mountain folds.

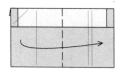

17. Valley fold in half.

18. Precrease along the angle bisector.

19. Open out along the center.

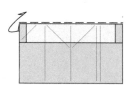

20. Raise the edge up from behind.

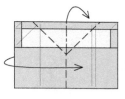

21. Fold in half while reverse folding along the existing creases.

22. Valley fold the flap over, allowing a small squash fold to form on the corner of the center hidden flap.

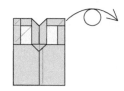

23. Turn over.

24. Valley fold the center flap over at the 1/3rd mark.

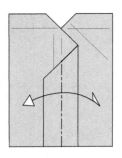

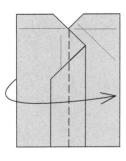

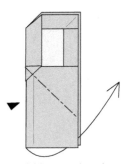

25. Precrease through all layers with a mountain fold.

26. Valley fold in half.

27. Reverse fold, spreading the layers evenly.

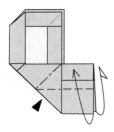

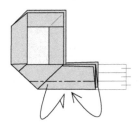

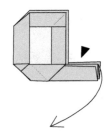

28. Fold the edges up, swivel folding in at each side.

29. Fold the edges in at each side at the 1/3rd mark.

30. Reverse fold, spreading the layers evenly.

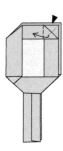

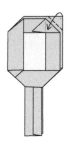

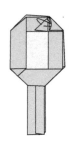

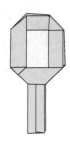

31. Squash fold the upper corner.

32. Valley fold the rear corner over the top section.

33. Tuck the flap into the pocket.

34. Completed *Tennis Racket.*

Baker

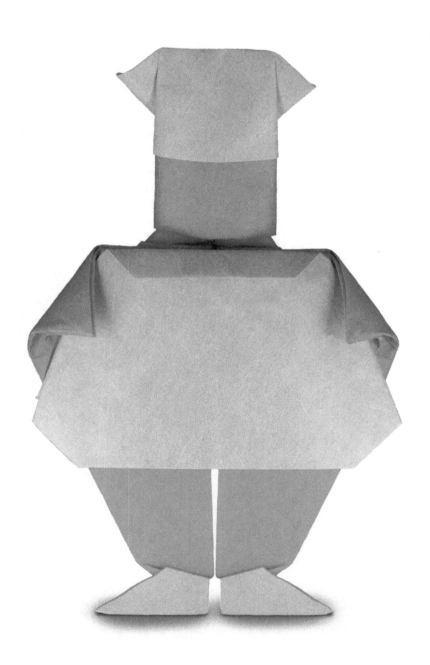

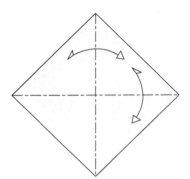

1. Precrease the diagonals with mountain folds.

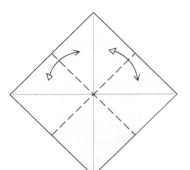

2. Precrease the sides in half.

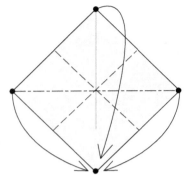

3. Collapse the corners down.

4. Precrease the sides along the angle bisectors.

5. Sink the top corner.

6. Valley fold to the top edge.

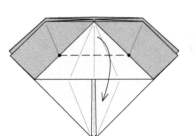

7. Valley fold using the dotted intersections of creases.

8. Valley fold the corner.

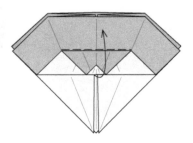

9. Swing the flap up.

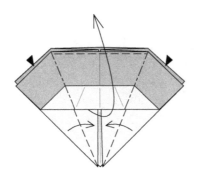

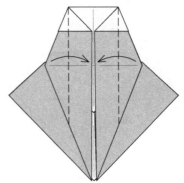

10. Mountain fold along the existing crease.

11. Petal fold the flap up.

12. Valley fold the corners to the center.

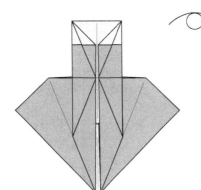

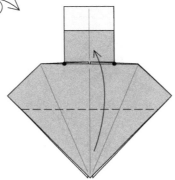

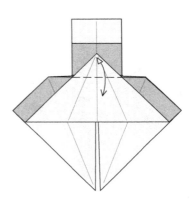

13. Turn over.

14. Valley fold the flap up so it hits the dotted corners.

15. Precrease to align with the folded edge below.

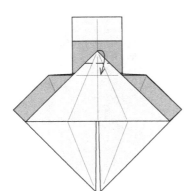

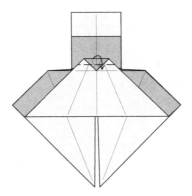

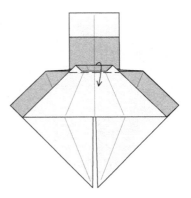

16. Valley fold to the last crease.

17. Valley fold the edge to the crease.

18. Valley fold along the existing crease.

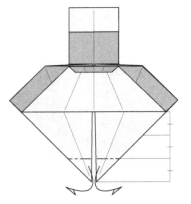

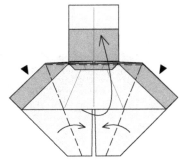

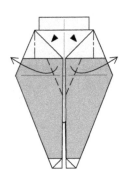

19. Mountain fold the corners at approximately 1/3rd the height if the flaps.

20. Petal fold the flap up.

21. Squash fold the sides outwards.

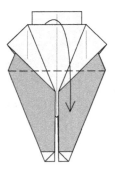

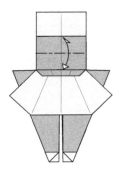

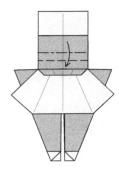

22. Valley fold the flap down.

23. Precrease the colored section in half with a mountain fold.

24. Pleat the top section down.

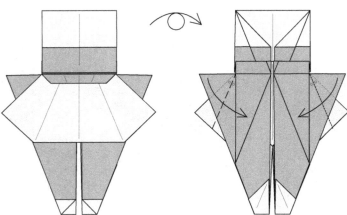

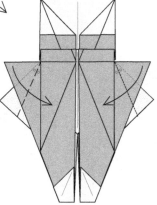

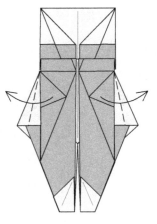

25. Turn over.

26. Valley fold the sides in along the indicated angle bisectors.

27. Valley fold the flaps outwards along the angle bisectors.

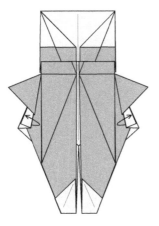

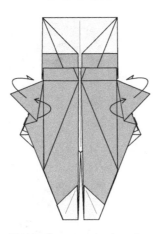

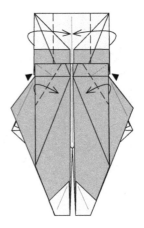

28. Release the trapped colored layer around to the surface at each side.

29. Flip the flaps over to the other side.

30. Valley fold the sides to the center, allowing squash folds to form at the pleated area.

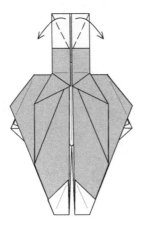

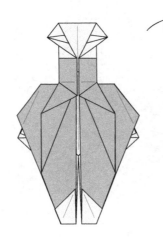

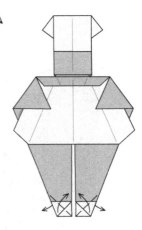

31. Valley fold the corners outwards.

32. Turn over.

33. Valley fold, allowing the flaps from behind to flip forward.

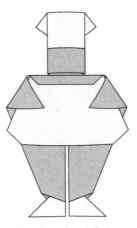

34. Completed *Baker*.

Building Block

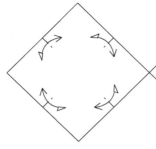

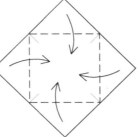

1. Precrease the edges in half.

2. Valley fold the corners to the center.

3. Precrease the edge in half.

4. Precrease at the area where the edges meet.

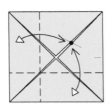

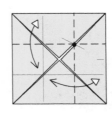

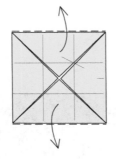

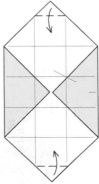

5. Precrease the side edges to meet the dotted intersection.

6. Precrease the opposite edges to meet the last creases.

7. Unfold the corners.

8. Valley fold along the existing creases.

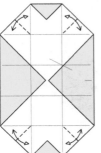

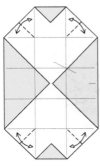

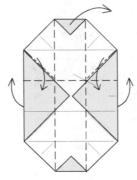

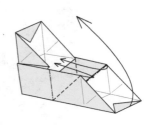

9. Precrease along the angle bisectors.

10. Precrease with mountain folds.

11. Crimp the side up, forming a 3-D shape.

12. Crimp the opposite side up.

13. Reverse fold the side down.

14. Reverse fold the opposite side down.

15. Tuck the flaps into the outer pockets.

16. Completed *Building Block*.

Television

1. Pinch the top edge in half.

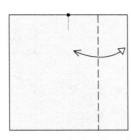

2. Precrease towards the dotted pinch mark.

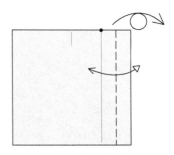

3. Precrease towards the dotted crease mark. Turn over.

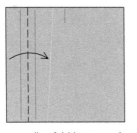

4. Form a valley fold between the two creases.

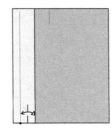

5. Form a pinch between the edge and the dotted crease.

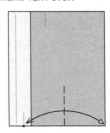

6. Precrease partway between the corner and the dotted crease.

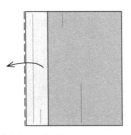

7. Unfold the side. Turn over.

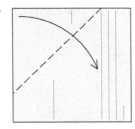

8. Valley fold towards the first crease.

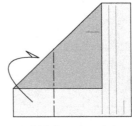

9. Mountain fold along the existing crease.

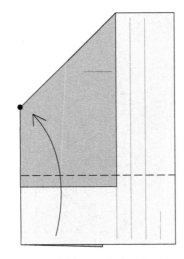

10. Valley fold towards the dotted corner.

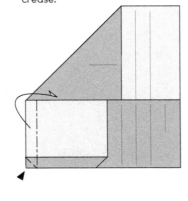

11. Swivel fold the edge inside.

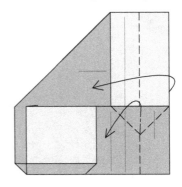

12. Valley fold while incorporating a reverse fold.

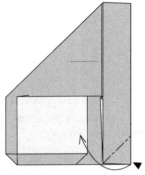

13. Reverse fold the corner.

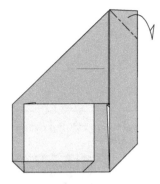

14. Mountain fold the corner.

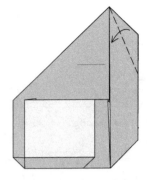

15. Valley fold along the angle bisector.

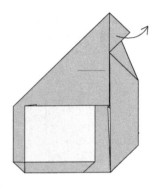

16. Unfold the pleat.

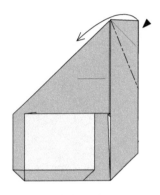

17. Reverse fold along the crease.

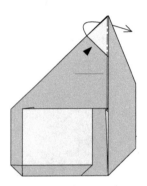

18. Reverse fold again.

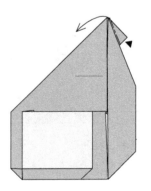

19. Reverse fold again.

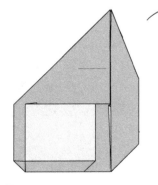

20. Turn over.

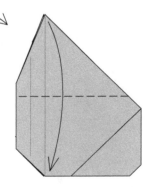

21. Valley fold in half.

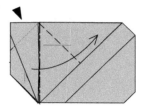

22. Squash fold the cluster of flaps.

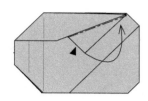

23. Reverse fold the corner.

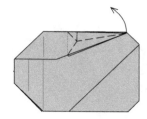

24. Rabbit ear the cluster of flaps.

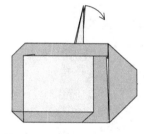

25. Turn over.

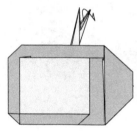

26. Open out the top two layers.

27. Mountain fold the layers behind.

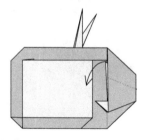

28. Slide the trapped point out.

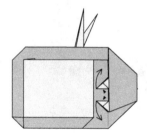

29. Wrap around a single layer.

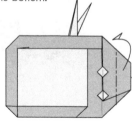

30. Reverse fold the flap, distributing one layer at the top and two at the bottom.

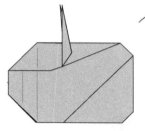

31. Valley fold the flap over.

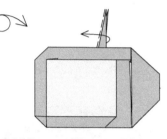

32. Squash fold the corners.

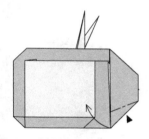

33. Mountain fold the edge.

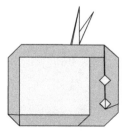

34. Completed *Television*.

Camera

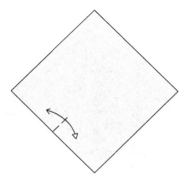

1. Precrease the edge in half.

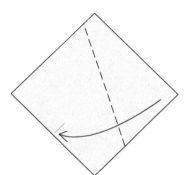

2. Valley fold the corner to the pinch mark.

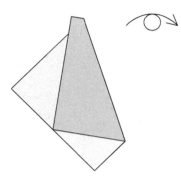

3. Turn over.

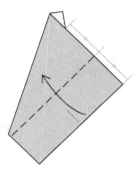

4. Valley fold so the corner hits the intersection.

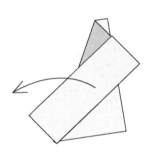

5. Unfold the pleat.

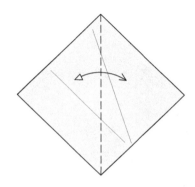

6. Precrease along the diagonal.

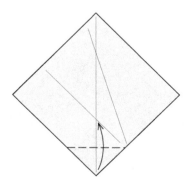

7. Valley fold the corner to the crease.

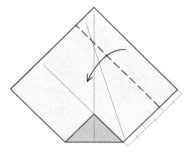

8. Valley fold the side in along 1/3rd its width.

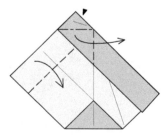

9. Valley fold the other side in to match, forming a squash fold at the top.

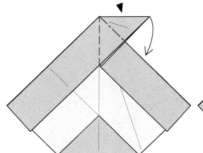

10. Squash fold the flap.

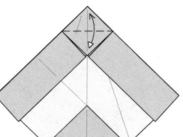

11. Precrease the top flap.

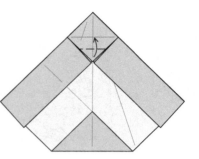

12. Valley fold to the last crease.

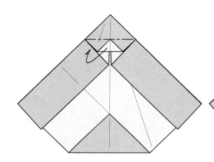

13. Tuck inside along the existing crease.

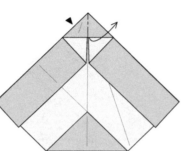

14. Open out the flap and squash fold flat.

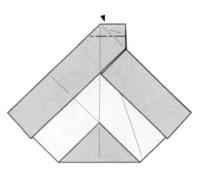

15. Sink the flap in half.

16. Valley fold the flap down, allowing its sides to spread apart flat.

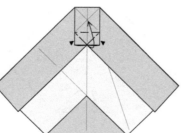

17. Petal fold the flap up.

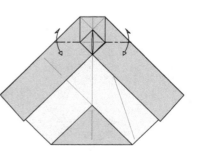

18. Precrease with a mountain fold.

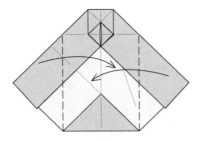

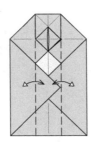

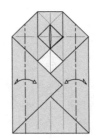

19. Valley fold the sides in, allowing them to overlap.

20. Lightly precrease the sides.

21. Precrease the sides with mountain folds.

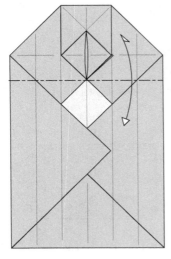

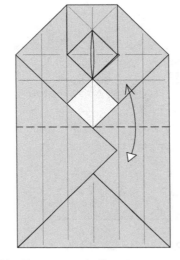

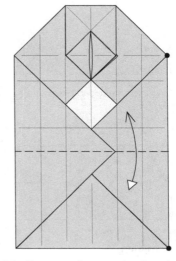

22. Precrease with a mountain fold.

23. Precrease in half.

24. Precrease between the dotted corners.

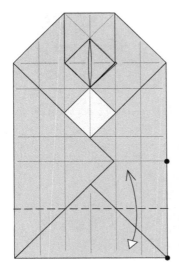

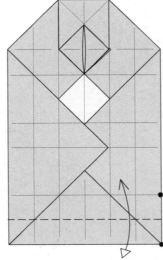

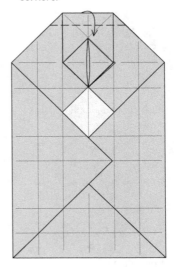

25. Precrease between the dotted corners.

26. Precrease between the dotted corners.

27. Valley found down.

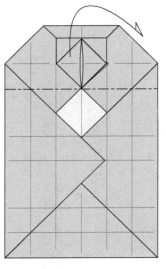

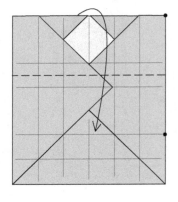

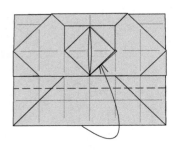

28. Mountain fold along the existing crease.

29. Lightly valley fold to the dotted crease.

30. Lightly valley fold, tucking underneath the center flap.

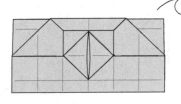

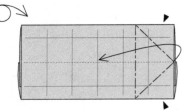

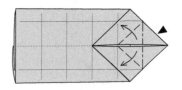

31. Turn over.

32. Petal fold to the center. Do not flatten the right side.

33. Squash fold the flap flat.

32-34

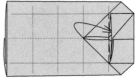

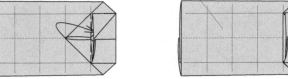

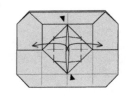

34. Tuck the flap into the pocket.

35. Repeat steps 32-34 on the other side in mirror image. Turn over.

36. Open out the sides and round them out.

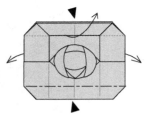

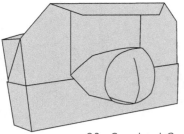

37. Raise the top flap slightly. Spread open the top and bottom, forming a boxlike shape.

38. Completed *Camera*.

Electric Guitar

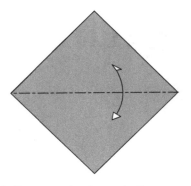

1. Precrease the diagonal with a mountain fold.

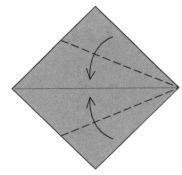

2. Valley fold the sides to the center.

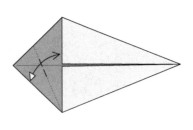

3. Pinch the center along the angle bisector.

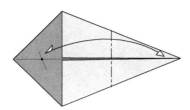

4. Precrease towards the dotted intersection with a mountain fold.

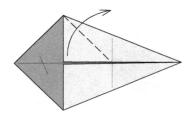

5. Valley fold up, aligning with the crease.

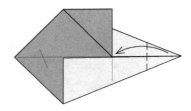

6. Lightly valley fold to the corner.

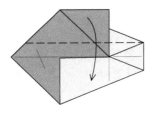

7. Valley fold the top section down.

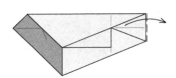

8. Swing over the side flap.

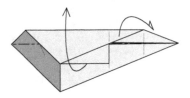

9. Flip the top section behind along the existing mountain fold.

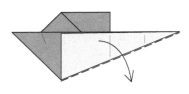

10. Open out the bottom flap.

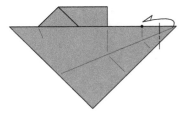

11. Mountain fold towards the dotted crease.

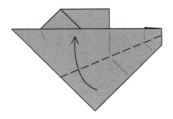

12. Valley fold the bottom edge back up.

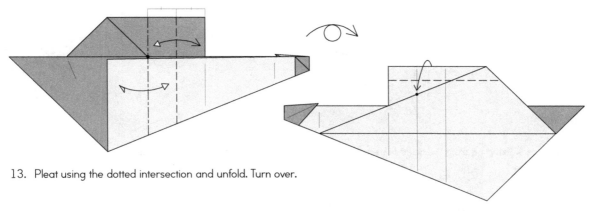

13. Pleat using the dotted intersection and unfold. Turn over.

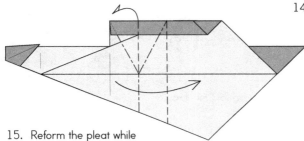

14. Valley fold towards the dotted intersection.

15. Reform the pleat while incorporating a reverse fold.

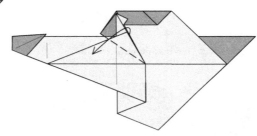

16. Open out the top flap.

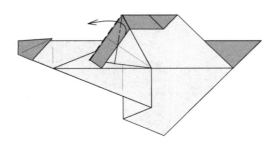

17. Slide over the trapped single layer and squash fold flat.

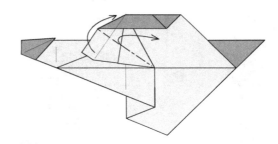

18. Swing the flap back up while squash folding the top layer.

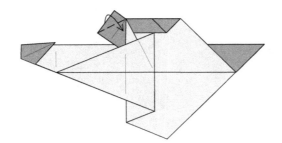

19. Valley fold the top layer.

20. Pull around the single layer to the surface.

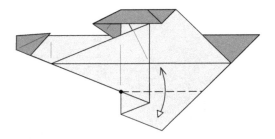

21. Precrease starting from the dotted intersection.

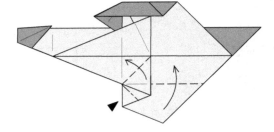

22. Squash fold the bottom edge.

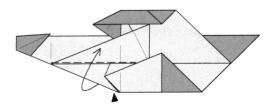

23. Reverse fold the bottom edge through.

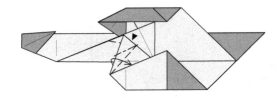

24. Squash fold the flap.

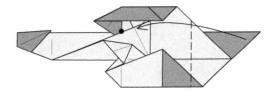

25. Valley fold towards the dotted intersection.

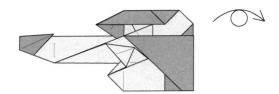

26. Turn over.

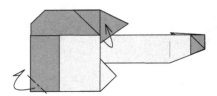

27. Mountain fold the corner. Bring the neck layer to the surface.

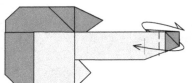

28. Valley fold, allowing the back flap to flip forward.

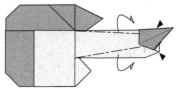

29. Mountain fold the sides allowing squash folds to form.

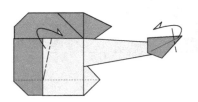

30. Mountain fold the indicated corners.

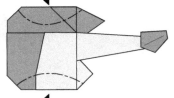

31. Push in the sides and round out the model to taste.

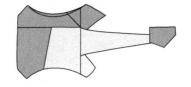

32. Completed *Electric Guitar*.

Matchbox

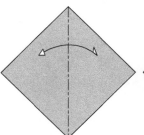

1. Precrease along the diagonal with a mountain fold.

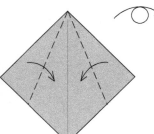

2. Valley fold the sides to the center. Turn over.

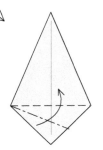

3. Pleat upwards.

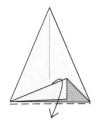

4. Swing down.

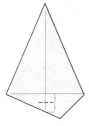

5. Precrease halfway.

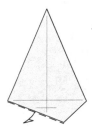

6. Open out. Turn over.

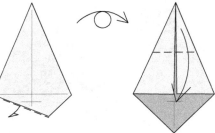

7. Valley fold to the precrease from step 4.

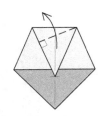

8. Valley fold upwards.

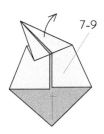

9. Unfold. Repeat steps 7-9 in mirror image.

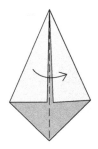

10. Valley fold in half.

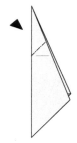

11. Reverse fold.

12. Outside reverse fold.

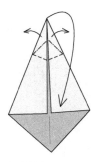
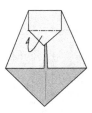

13. Undo the reverse folds.

14. Squash fold the top using the existing creases.

15. Mountain fold.

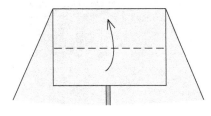
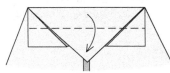
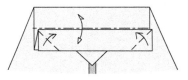

16. Valley fold lightly. Allow the flap folded in the previous step to flip out.

17. Valley fold in half.

18. Precrease with a mountain fold. Valley fold the top corners up.

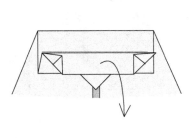
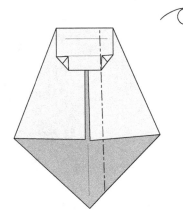
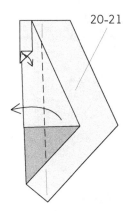

19. Unfold the pleat.

20. Mountain fold, using the tiny folded corner as a guideline. Turn over.

21. Undo the tiny valley fold. Valley fold outwards along the center of the model. Repeat steps 20-21 in mirror image.

20-21

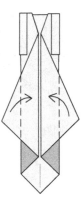

22. Valley fold towards the center.

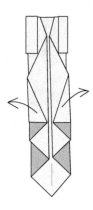

23. If the center corners overlap, you will have to reverse them outwards at step 30. Unfold the pleats.

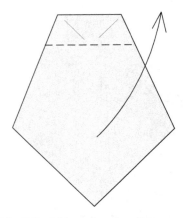

24. Valley fold up along the existing crease.

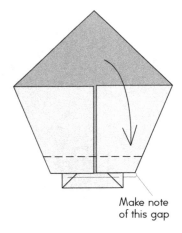

Make note of this gap

25. Valley fold down, such that the indicated gap is the same as the gap indicated in the next step.

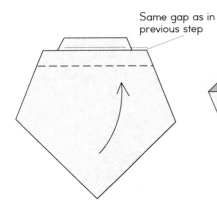

Same gap as in previous step

26. Valley fold up to meet the folded edge underneath.

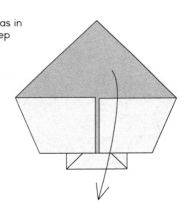

27. Open out the pleats.

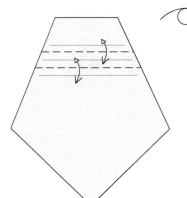

28. Precrease by inserting valley folds. Turn over.

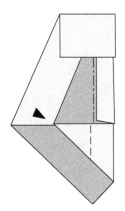

29. Closed reverse fold along the existing crease.

30. Reverse fold along the existing crease.

29-31

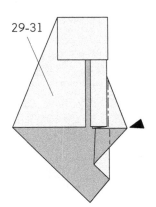

31. Reverse fold again. If the corner extends beyond the center, reverse fold it outwards to make the center edges flush. Repeat steps 29-31 in mirror image.

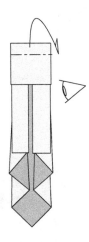

32. Mountain fold at 90 degrees along the existing crease.

33. View from the previous step. Pull out the center layer to lie at 90 degrees.

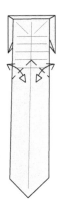

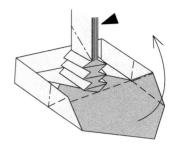

34. Repeat step 33 on the other side.

35. Precrease.

36. Add additional folds (at roughly 90 degrees to each other) to create a pleat.

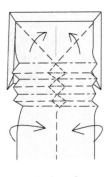

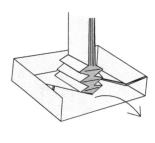

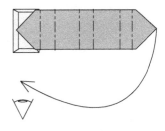

37. Rabbit ear the long flap straight up. Allow the pleats to collapse. New folds will form on the top single layer automatically.

38. Pull out the single layer.

39. Squash fold the top flap along the existing creases. Collapse the front as indicated.

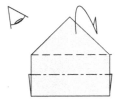

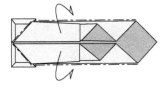

40. Front view. Tuck the flap in (under the pleated section).

41. View from step 40. Wrap all the layers around to create a color change.

42. Wrap the flap around the box.

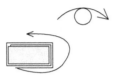

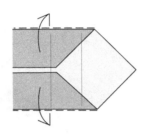

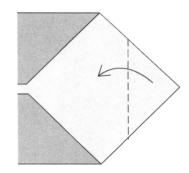

43. View from step 42. Unwrap the flap and turn over.

44. The end of the flap is pictured. Open out the sides (the model will not lie flat).

45. Valley fold along the existing crease.

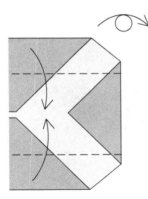

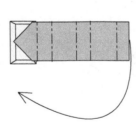

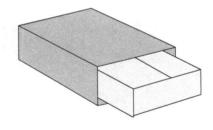

46. Valley fold the sides back in. Turn over.

47. Using the existing creases, tuck the flap into itself. Work from the center towards the outside edges, pushing the inner box from side to side to gain access. Smoothing out the inside will improve the mechanism.

48. Completed *Matchbox*.

Skier

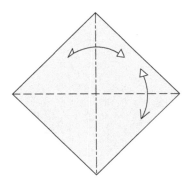

1. Precrease the diagonals with mountain and valley folds.

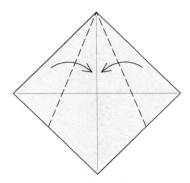

2. Valley fold the sides to the center.

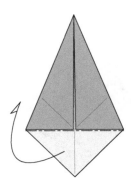

3. Mountain fold the corner behind.

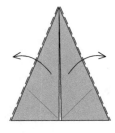

4. Open out the sides.

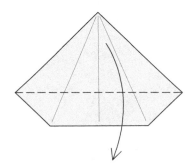

5. Valley fold down.

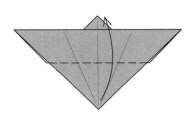

6. Valley fold up to meet the top corner.

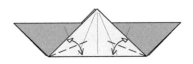

7. Precrease along the angle bisectors.

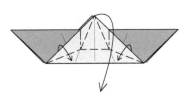

8. Fold the flap down while swivel folding in the sides.

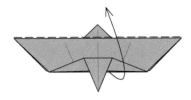

9. Open out along the center.

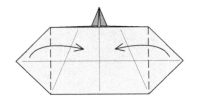

10. Valley fold the corners.

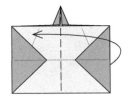

11. Valley fold in half.

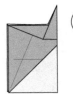

12. Rotate the model.

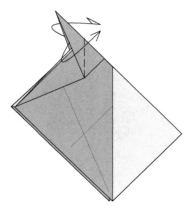

13. Outside reverse fold the top flap.

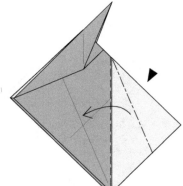

14. Squash fold the flap over.

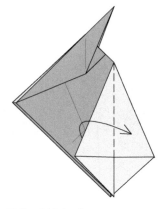

15. Valley fold the flap over.

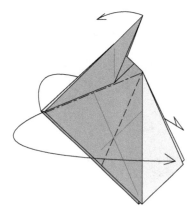

16. Crimp the sides so the left corners meet the right corners.

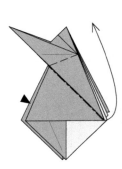

17. Squash fold the top flap. The original corner will pop out.

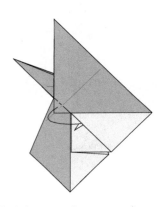

18. Tuck the original corner inside.

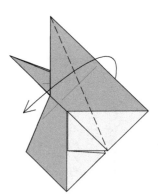

19. Valley fold the top flap.

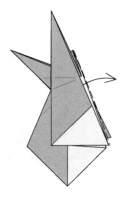

20. Pull out the trapped single layer and flatten.

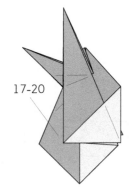

21. Repeat steps 17-20 behind.

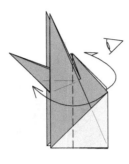

22. Spread apart the side flap. Do not crease sharply.

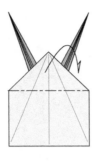

23. View from the previous step. Mountain fold the corner inside.

24. Close the flap back up while incorporating a reverse fold.

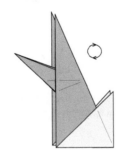

25. Rotate the model slightly.

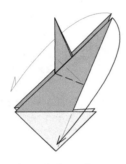

26. Swing the side flaps down.

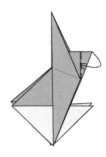

27. Tuck the corner inside.

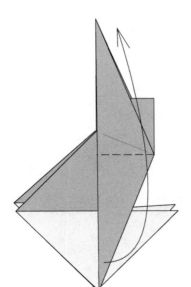

28. Valley fold the flap up.

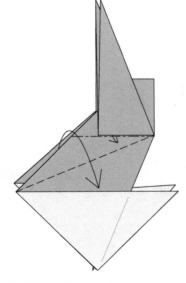

29. Valley fold along the angle bisector, pulling out some paper from underneath the flap.

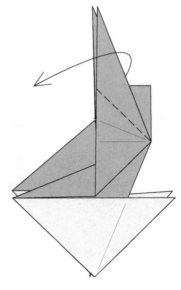

30. Valley fold so the top edge lies straight.

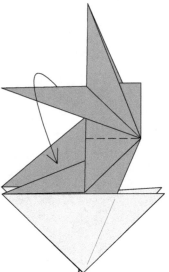

31. Swing the flap down.

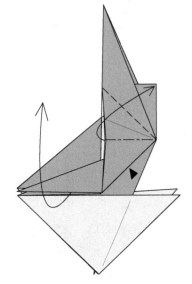

32. Bring the flap back up while pulling two layers over and squash folding flat.

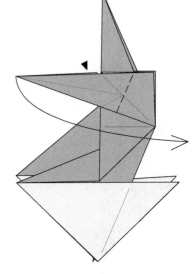

33. Valley fold the flap over while squash folding the inside layers.

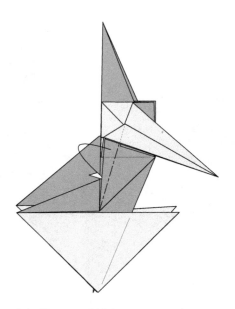

34. Mountain fold the top trapped edge inside.

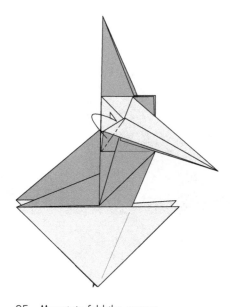

35. Mountain fold the corner.

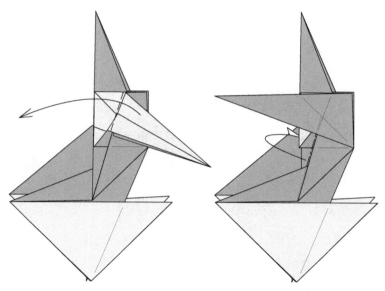

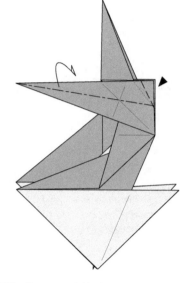

36. Swing the flap back over.

37. Tuck the remaining layers inside.

38. Mountain fold along the angle bisector while swivel folding at the corner.

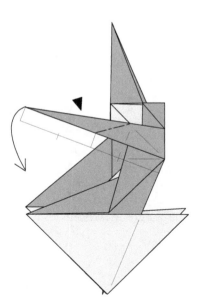

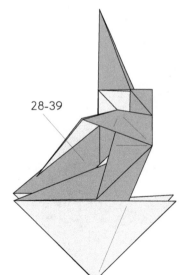

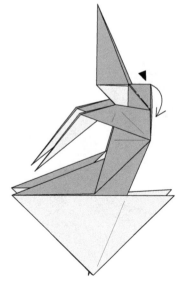

39. Reverse fold the flap, distributing the layers evenly to reveal the inner color.

40. Repeat steps 28-39 on the other side.

28-39

41. Reverse fold the corner.

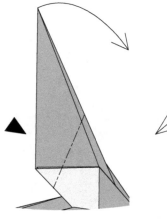
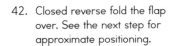

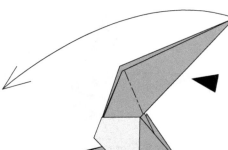

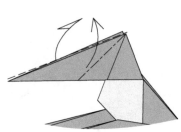

42. Closed reverse fold the flap over. See the next step for approximate positioning.

43. Reverse fold the flap through.

44. Slide the layers up at each side.

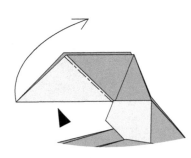

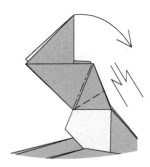

45. Reverse fold the corner up.

46. Crimp the top section down.

47. Mountain fold the corners inside.

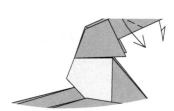

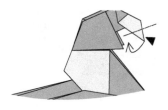

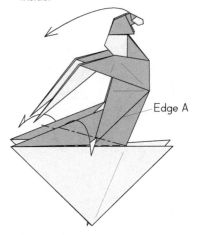

Edge A

48. Outside reverse fold the flap.

49. Reverse fold the tip of the flap.

50. Crimp the top section over so Edge A can extend to meet the bottom corner. See step 53 for this alignment.

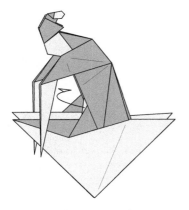

51. Swivel fold the protruding middle layer inside.

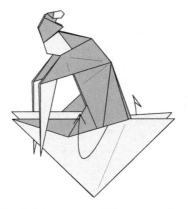

52. Pull the outer single layer around to the surface at each side.

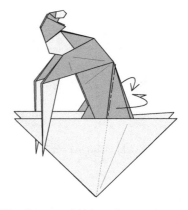

53. Mountain fold the edges inside.

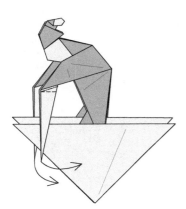

54. Pleat the flaps so they tilt inwards.

55. Open out the bottom side flaps allowing a squash fold to form on the middle layer.

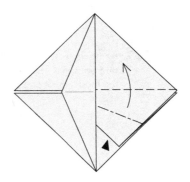

56. View from the previous step. Squash fold the center flap.

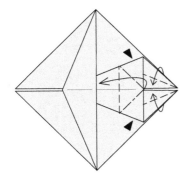

57. Petal fold the flap.

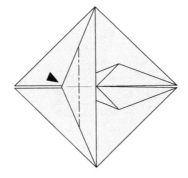

58. Sink the tip of the flap about halfway.

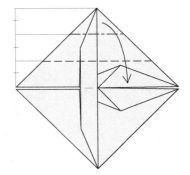

59. Pleat the flap inwards using equal divisions.

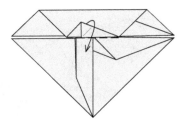

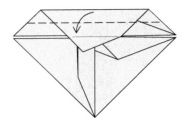

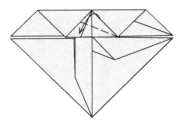

60. Valley fold along the angle bisector.

61. Swing the flap down.

62. Valley fold the flap up at a 90 degree angle.

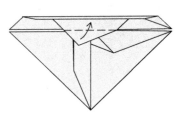

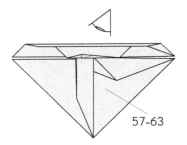

63. Swing the flap up at a 90 degree angle. This flap allows the model to sit at a slight incline.

64. Repeat steps 57-63 on the bottom flap.

57-63

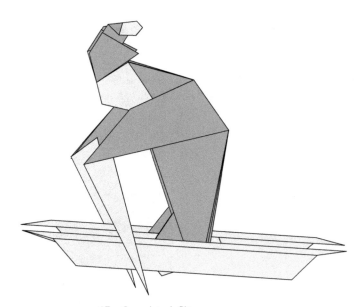

65. Completed *Skier*.

Golfer

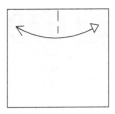

1. Pinch the top edge in half.

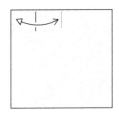

2. Pinch again.

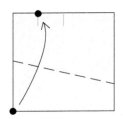

3. Valley fold the dotted corner to the crease.

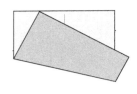

4. Turn over.

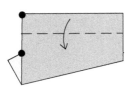

5. Valley fold to the intersection of raw edges.

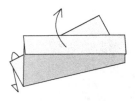

6. Unfold.

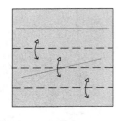

7. Precrease the lower section into fourths.

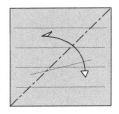

8. Precrease along the diagonal with a mountain fold.

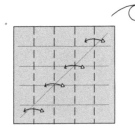

9. Precrease into fifths. Use the intersections of the diagonal crease as a guide. Turn over.

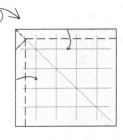

10. Valley fold the side edges to the creases, forming a rabbit ear at the corner.

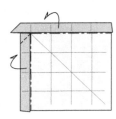

11. Mountain fold along the existing creases, swivel folding behind.

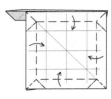

12. Valley fold the sides inwards, allowing swivel folds to form.

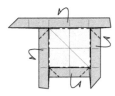

13. Mountain fold along the existing creases, swivel folding behind.

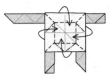

14. Valley fold the sides inwards, allowing swivel folds to form.

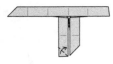

15. Valley fold the corner.

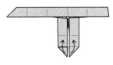

16. Valley fold the flaps up.

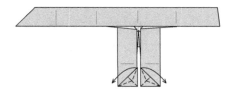

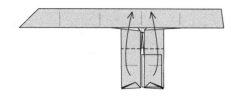

17. Rabbit ear the flaps outwards.

18. Valley fold the flaps up, to align with the folded edge in the rear.

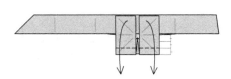

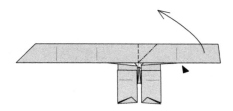

19. Valley fold the flaps down at approximately 1/3rd the indicated distance.

20. Squash fold the flap up.

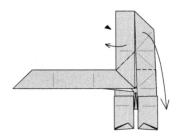

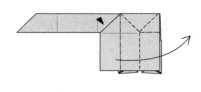

21. Open out the side while valley folding down.

22. Rabbit ear the flap outwards.

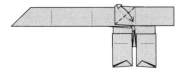

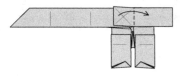

23. Precrease the center flap.

24. Valley fold the center flap over.

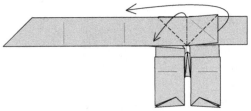

25. Swing over the center flap while incorporating a reverse fold.

26. Spread squash the center flap down.

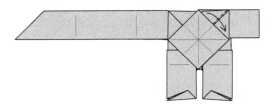

27. Valley fold the flap down.

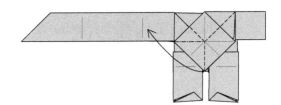

28. Rabbit ear the center flap.

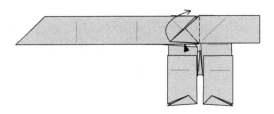

29. Squash fold.

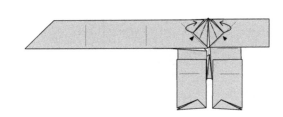

30. Reverse fold the sides.

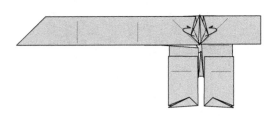

31. Mountain fold the sides.

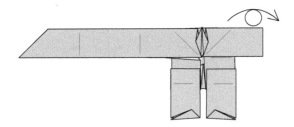

32. Turn over.

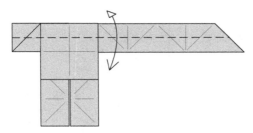

33. Precrease the top edge in half.

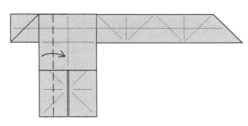

34. Valley fold the side edge over.

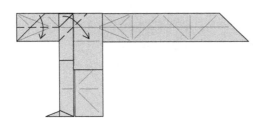

35. Precrease along the angle bisectors.

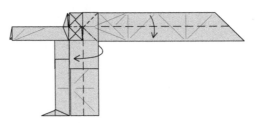

36. Precrease along the angle bisectors.

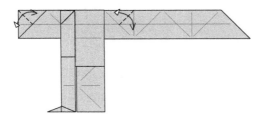

37. Valley fold the thick center flap over while valley folding the left flap in half.

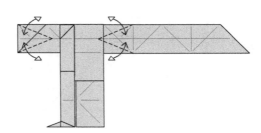

38. Valley fold the two flaps in half, allowing a swivel fold to form.

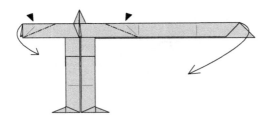

39. Reverse fold along the existing creases.

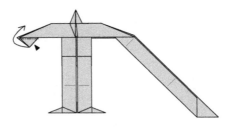

40. Reverse fold the corner up.

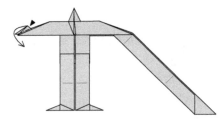

41. Reverse fold the corner down.

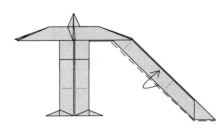

42. Wrap around a single layer.

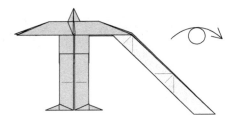

43. Turn over.

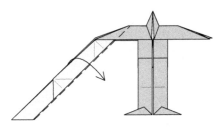

44. Open out the top layer. The tip will not lie flat.

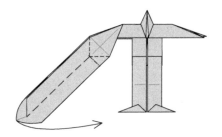

45. Rabbit ear the flap down to flatten.

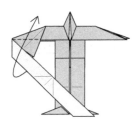

46. Valley fold the flap up.

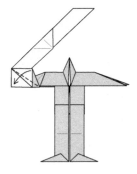

47. Valley fold the corner over.

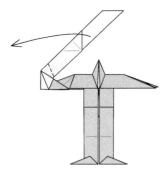

48. Valley fold the flap over so it lies straight.

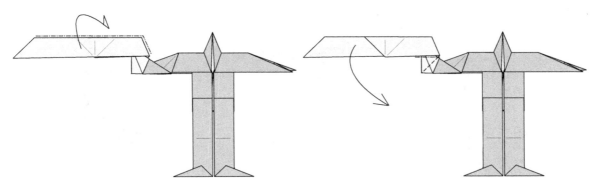

49. Wrap around a single layer.

50. Pleat the flap downwards.

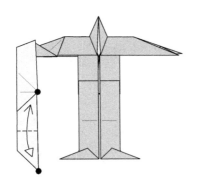

51. Precrease the flap.

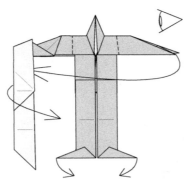

52. Open out the flaps for the feet. Tuck one of the points into the pocket.

53. View from the previous step. Mountain fold the tips of the flaps for the feet.

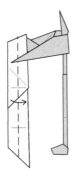

54. Valley fold the flap in half, locking the arm in place.

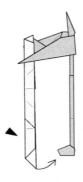

55. Form a reverse fold, using the crease from step 51 as a guide.

56. Reverse fold the flap through.

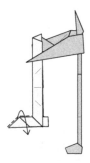 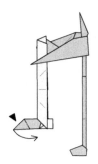 

57. Wrap around a single layer, allowing a swivel fold to form internally.

58. Reverse fold the tip.

59. Open out the sides.

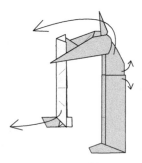 

60. Spread apart the side pleats and pull the body and club into position.

61. Open out the sides of the head and round the sides of the body.

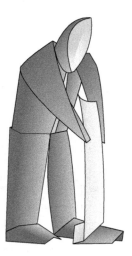

62. Completed *Golfer*.

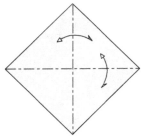

1. Precrease with mountain folds.

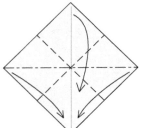

2. Collapse down.

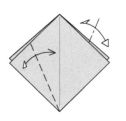

3. Precrease along the angle bisectors.

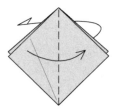

4. Swing a flap over at each side.

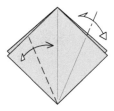

5. Precrease along the angle bisectors.

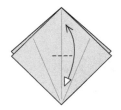

6. Pinch the center of the top flap.

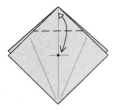

7. Precrease to the pinch.

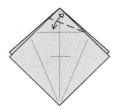

8. Precrease along the angle bisector.

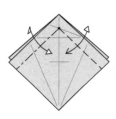

9. Precrease with mountain and valley folds, avoiding creasing at the tip.

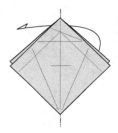

10. Swing one flap over.

11. Swivel fold up the top layer.

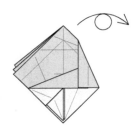

12. Turn over.

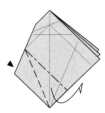

13. Swivel fold under to match the other side.

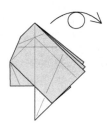

14. Turn over.

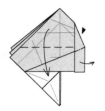

15. Squash fold the top down.

16. Precrease through all layers.

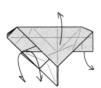

17. Open out.

18. Swing over a flap at each side.

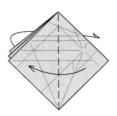

11-18
×3

19. Repeat steps 11-18 three times.

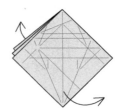

20. Unfold completely.

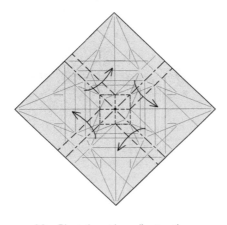

21. Pleat the sides, allowing the center to twist upwards.

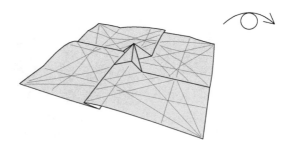

22. Turn over.

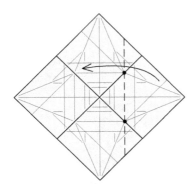

23. Valley fold through the indicated intersections.

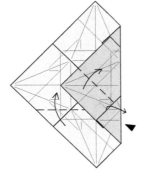

24. Swivel fold the flap over, using similar intersections on the other side.

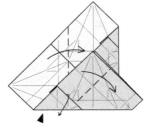

25. Swivel fold again.

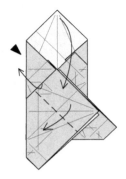

26. Swivel fold again.

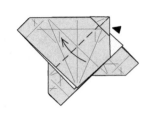

27. Squash fold.

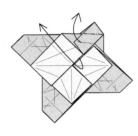

28. Pull out the hidden corner.

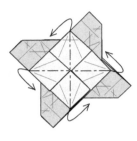

29. Raise the four center flaps, bringing the corners together.

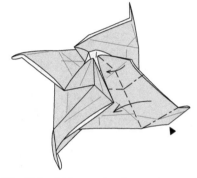

30. Valley fold inwards, allowing the outer portion to squash fold flat.

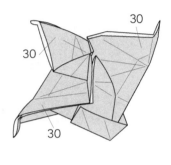

31. Repeat step 30 on the remaining three sides.

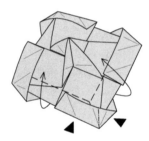

32. Valley fold the edges up while squash folding the corner flat.

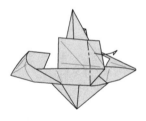

33. Mountain fold so that the flap is flush with the sides.

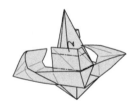

34. Mountain fold over and over, which will lock the corner into place.

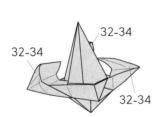

35. Repeat steps 32-34 on the remaining three corners.

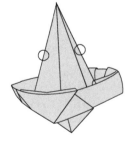

36. Hold by the indicated outside edges and spin.

37. Completed *Top*.

Fluffy (Teddy Bear)

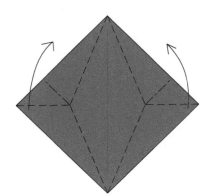

1. With the darker side up, form rabbit ears on both sides.

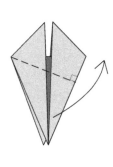

2. Swing the flap back.

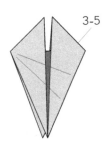

3. Valley fold up.

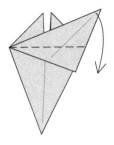

4. Valley fold down.

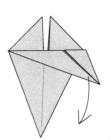

5. Unfold the pleat.

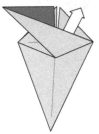

3-5

6. Repeat steps 3-5 in mirror image.

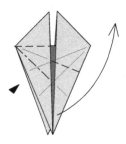

7. Form an asymmetrical squash fold.

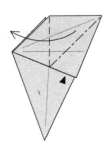

8. Squash fold.

9. Pull out a single layer to match the other side.

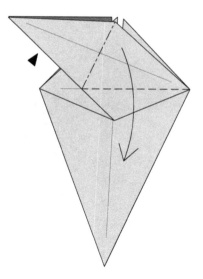

10. Squash fold.

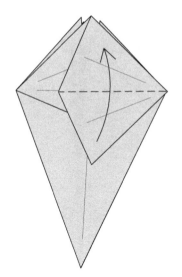

11. Valley fold up.

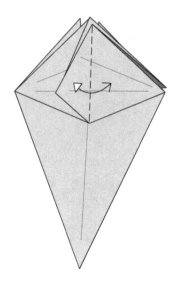

12. Precrease the center flap.

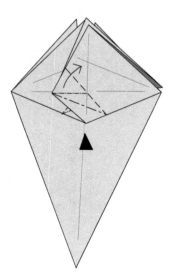

13. Form a valley fold, allowing a squash fold to form at the bottom.

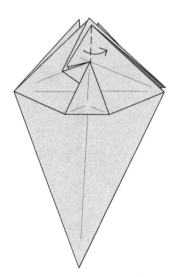

14. Pull one layer through.

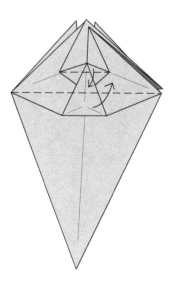

15. Form two valley folds.

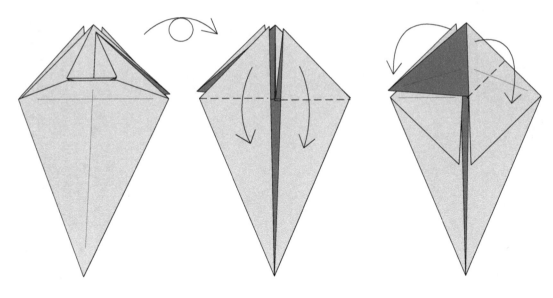

16. Turn over.

17. Swing the top flaps down.

18. Open out the top.

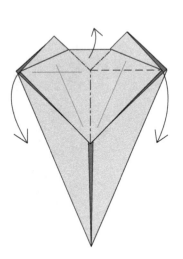

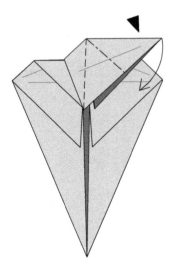

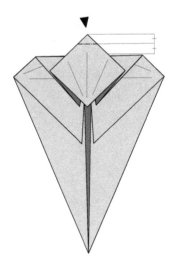

19. Collapse into a rabbit-ear formation.

20. Squash fold the center flap.

21. Sink halfway.

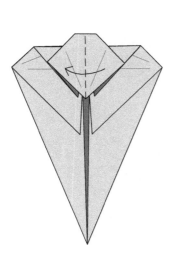

22. Swing over.

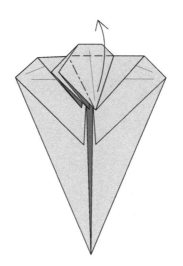

23. Petal fold up.

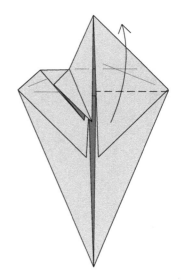

24. Swing up.

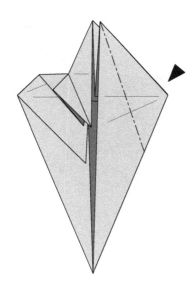

25. Sink triangularly.

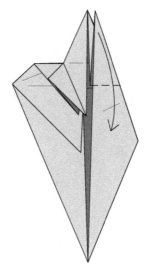

26. Swing down.

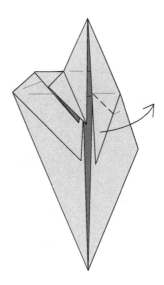

27. Valley fold outwards.

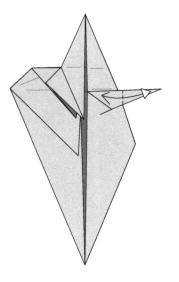

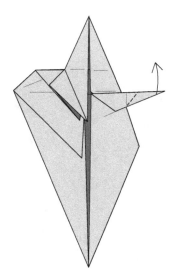

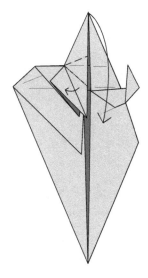

28. Precrease the flap halfway.

29. Valley fold to lie along the precrease.

30. Valley fold the top flap down while swinging out the top single layer.

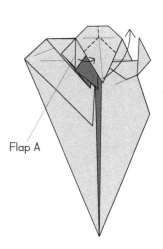

Flap A

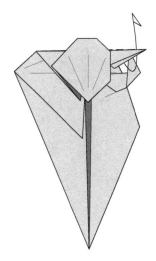

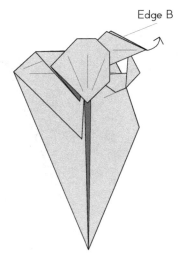

Edge B

31. Swing over flap A, while incorporating a reverse fold. A gusset will form where flap A meets the point.

32. Pull up the thick set of layers

33. Pull up edge B so that it lies straight.

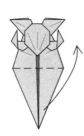

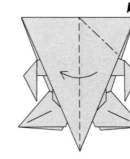

34. Repeat steps 22-33 in mirror image.

35. Valley fold. Rotate the model.

36. Squash fold.

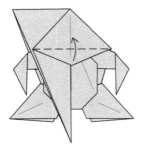

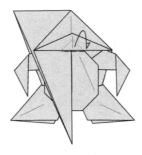

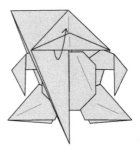

37. Valley fold up.

38. Mountain fold the single layer to match up with folded edge above.

39. Wrap around a single layer from underneath.

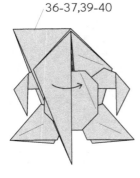

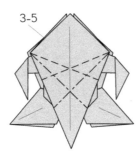

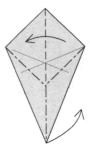

40. Swing over. Repeat steps 36-40 on the other side, skipping step 38.

41. Repeat steps 3-5 on the top flap.

42. The top flap is shown only. Fold in half while outside reverse folding.

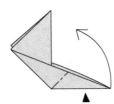

43. Reverse fold.

44. Wrap around a single layer from underneath.

45. Repeat step 44 behind (it is easier to first swing the small flap to the other side to accomplish this).

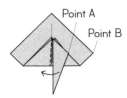

46. Swing one flap over.

47. Valley fold up. See the next step for positioning.

48. Note that points A and B are on the same plane. Swing over.

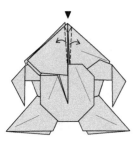

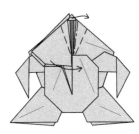

49. Swing over.

50. Fold out the top edges a small amount, allowing the tip to squash fold.

51. Swing over the head while swivel folding out the ear. Form the mountain fold first. The center of the ear should lie at a 45° angle.

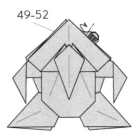

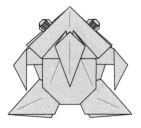

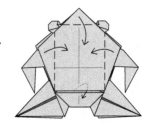

52. Mountain fold the edge of the ear to make it symmetrical. Repeat steps 49-52 in mirror image.

53. Turn over.

54. Valley fold the sides in. Pull out the tiny flap from the bottom pocket.

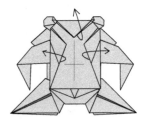

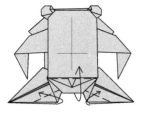

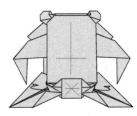

55. Pull a single layer to the surface (closed sink). The sides can be reverse folded instead.

56. Stretch the bottom upwards. Valley fold the lower edges of the legs to the center.

57. Swivel fold the layers from the legs behind.

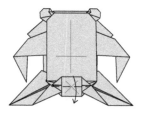

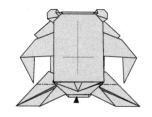

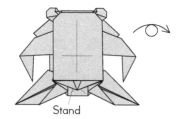

58. Swing down.

59. Closed sink.

60. Note the flap for the stand. Turn over.

Stand

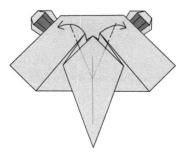

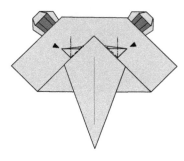

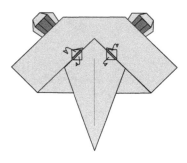

61. Reverse fold.

62. Squash fold the tiny flaps.

63. Wrap a single layer around each side to color change.

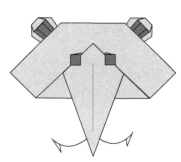

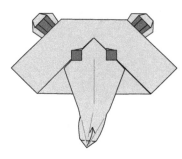

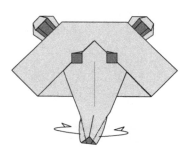

64. Spread out the tip of the nose.

65. Valley fold the tip up.

66. Mountain fold the side layers of the nose back in.

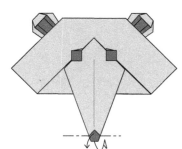

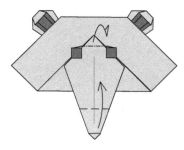

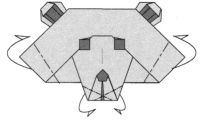

67. Flip the colored layer of the nose down.

68. Mountain fold the top corner. Valley fold the nose up.

69. Shape the head to taste with mountain folds.

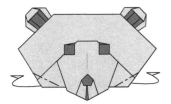

70. More shaping.

71. Completed head.

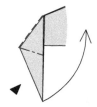

72. Squash fold the arm.

73. Swing down while spreading out the top layers.

74. Valley fold over.

75. Valley fold the edges in (fold the bottom one first).

76. Mountain fold the tip.

77. Completed arm. Repeat steps 72-76 on the other arm.

78. Mountain fold the top edge of leg to match the bottom edge.

79. Pull out layers from the sides to make the leg 3-D.

80. Wrap the corner over.

81. Completed leg. Repeat steps 78-80 on the other leg. Stretch the stand (see step 60) down. Stretch the legs forward and round the model to taste.

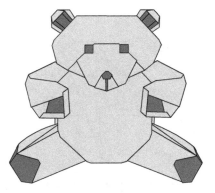

82. Completed *Fluffy (Teddy Bear)*.

Jack-in-the-box

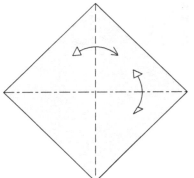

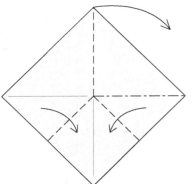

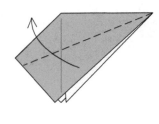

1. Precrease the diagonals with both a valley fold and a mountain fold.

2. Rabbit ear.

3. Valley fold along the angle bisector.

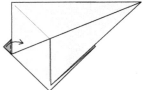

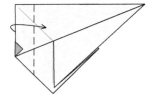

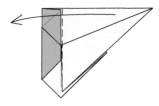

4. Valley fold the protruding corner.

5. Valley fold to the center.

6. Valley fold the large flap over.

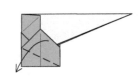

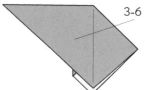

7. Repeat steps 3-6 in mirror image.

8. Lightly valley fold up.

9. Lightly valley fold down.

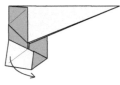

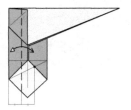

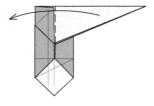

10. Unfold the pleat.

11. Precrease over to the dotted intersection.

12. Swing over the center flap.

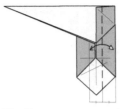

13. Precrease over to the existing crease.

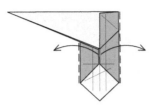

14. Swing the side flaps outwards.

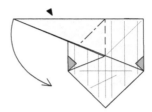

15. Squash fold the center flap.

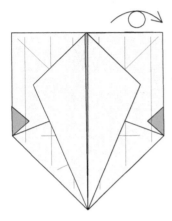

16. Turn over.

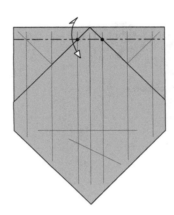

17. Precrease through the dotted intersection of creases.

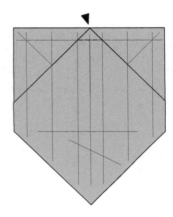

18. Sink the trapped point. You will have to open up the model to do this.

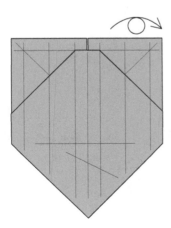

19. Turn over.

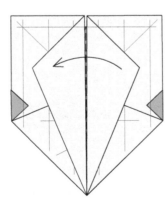

20. Swing over the large flap.

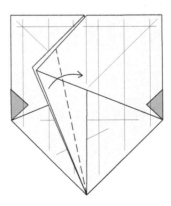

21. Valley fold along the angle bisector.

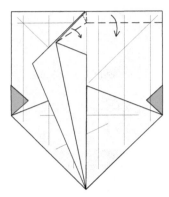

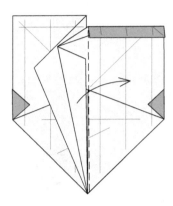

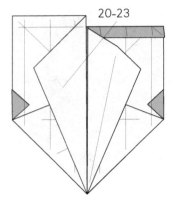

20-23

22. Valley fold along the crease, allowing a pleat to form.

23. Open out the pleat.

24. Repeat steps 20-23 in mirror image.

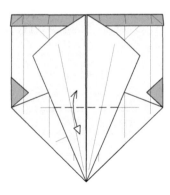

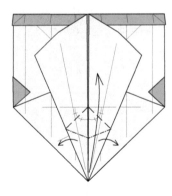

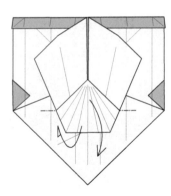

25. Precrease to match the crease beneath.

26. Forming the angle bisector folds first, squash fold the top flap.

27. Flip the flap along its corners.

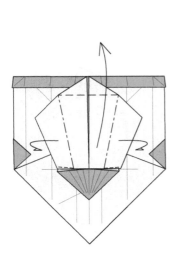

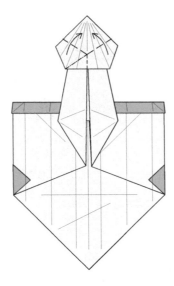

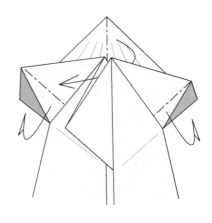

28. Petal fold upwards, allowing the sides to swivel fold in.

29. Rabbit ear as far as possible.

30. Form mountain folds along the arms, and then pull the head through the pocket.

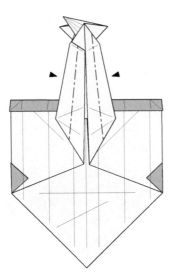

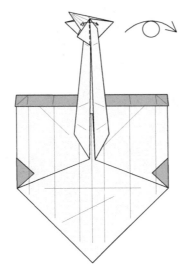

31. Sink the sides in triangularly.

32. Precrease the center flap. Turn over.

33. Spread apart the center point, and squash fold using the existing creases.

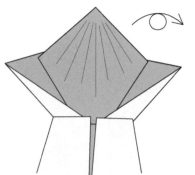

34. Turn over.

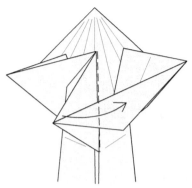

35. Valley fold over and over.

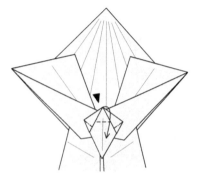

36. Swing over the center flap.

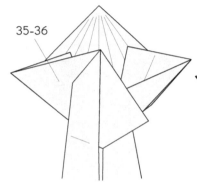

37. Repeat steps 35-36 in mirror image.

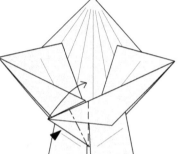

38. Squash fold the center flap.

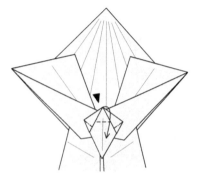

39. Squash fold the flap again.

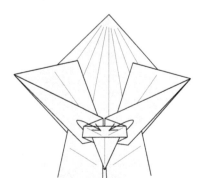

40. Pull the layers from the arms to the surface.

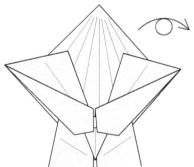

41. Turn over.

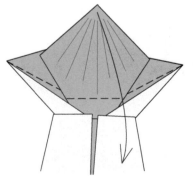

42. Stretch the top flap down as far as possible.

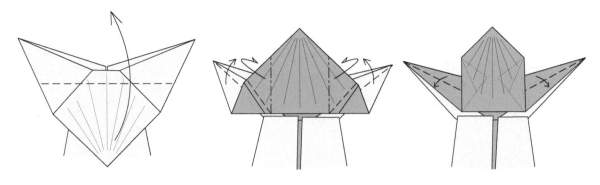

43. Valley fold up.

44. Swivel fold in the sides.

45. Valley fold the top layer of the arms, allowing a swivel fold to form behind.

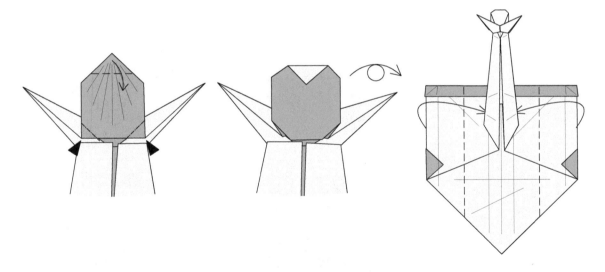

46. Sink the corners and valley fold the top.

47. Completed head. Turn over.

48. Valley fold the flaps to the center, tucking them under the center flap.

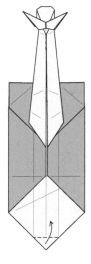

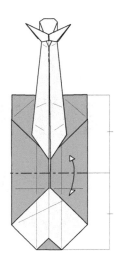

49. Valley fold the bottom corner up from where it hits the crease lines.

50. Precrease in half with a mountain fold.

51. Precrease where indicated.

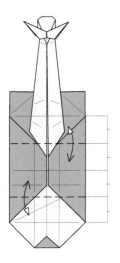

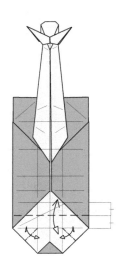

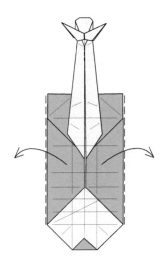

52. Precrease at the indicated divisions.

53. Add more precreases.

54. Open out the sides again.

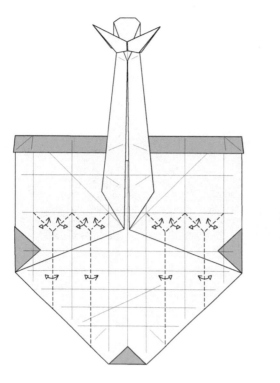

55. Form the indicated precreases with valley folds.

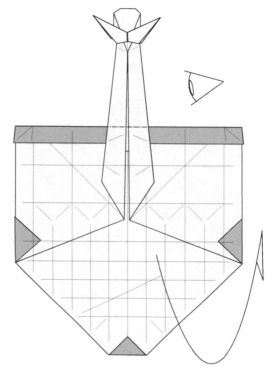

56. Form a mountain fold, such that the two sections lie at 90° from each other.

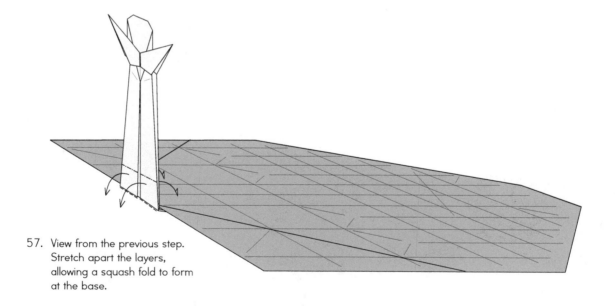

57. View from the previous step. Stretch apart the layers, allowing a squash fold to form at the base.

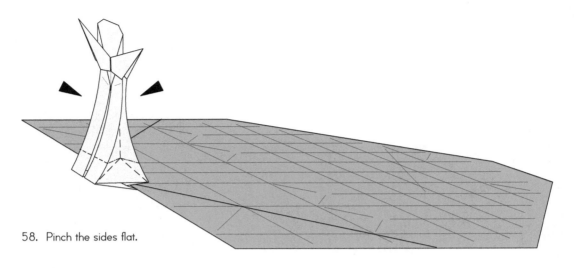

58. Pinch the sides flat.

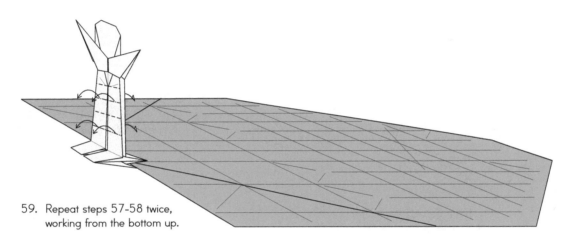

59. Repeat steps 57-58 twice,
    working from the bottom up.

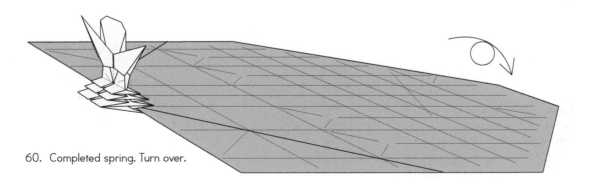

60. Completed spring. Turn over.

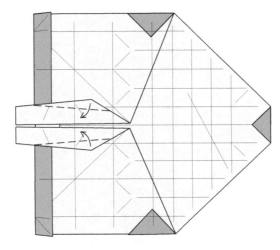

61. Valley fold the sides in.

62. Swivel fold over, forming a boxlike shape.

63. Tuck the hem under the flap.

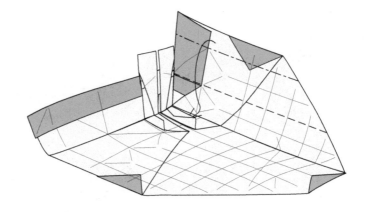

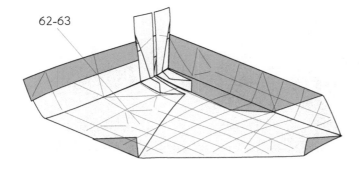

62-63

64. Repeat steps 62-63 on the other side.

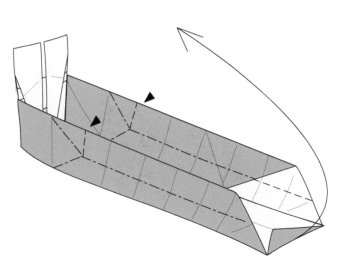

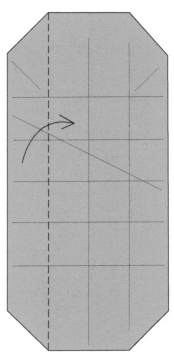

65. Double rabbit ear both sides, distributing the layers as evenly as possible.

66. Valley fold to the center.

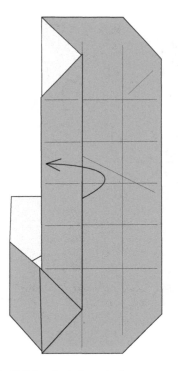

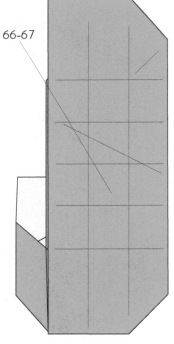

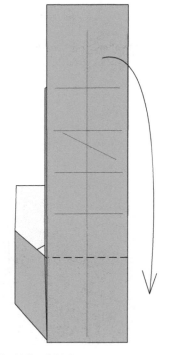

66-67

67. Pull the single layer to the surface (closed sink).

68. Repeat 66-67 on the other side.

69. Valley fold down.

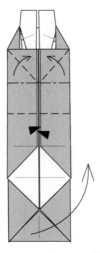

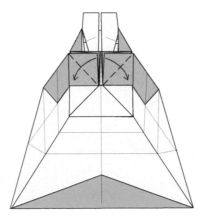

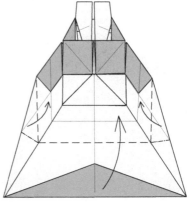

70. Push the center edges out flat, while swivel folding at the top.

71. Valley fold the corners down.

72. Bring the bottom upwards, while forming reverse folds to lie along the sides.

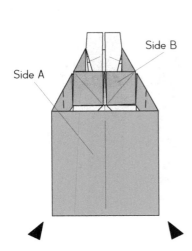

Side A   Side B

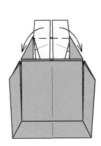

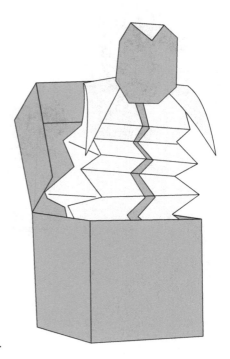

73. Using the existing creases, invert side A to lie on side B.

74. Pull the set of pleats towards the back of the box. Position the arms, pleats and lid to taste.

75. Completed *Jack-in-the-box*.

Chess Pieces

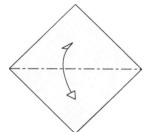

1. Precrease with a
   mountain fold.

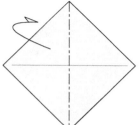

2. Mountain fold in half.

3. Precrease the lower
   portion.

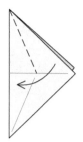

4. Valley fold part way. The
   model will not lie flat.

5. Squash fold to flatten.

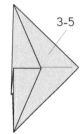

3-5

6. Repeat steps 3-5
   behind.

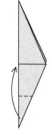

7. Valley fold to the center.

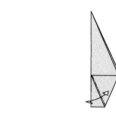

8. Precrease with a
   mountain fold.

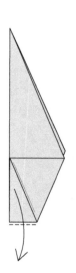

9. Unfold.

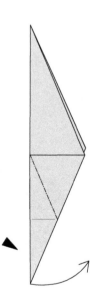

10. Reverse fold.

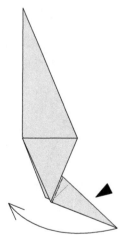

11. Reverse fold again.

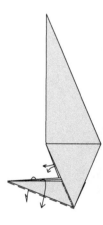

12. Pull out a single layer
    at each side.

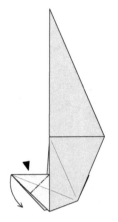

13. Reverse fold.

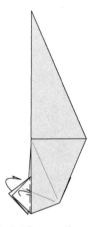

14. Tuck the flaps under the outer layers.

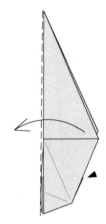

15. Open out, allowing the center flap to squash fold flat.

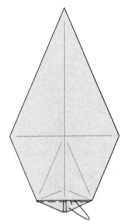

16. Valley fold into the pocket.

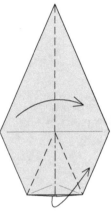

17. Valley fold over while incorporating a reverse fold.

18. Reverse fold the center layer through.

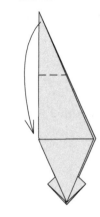

19. Valley fold to the corner.

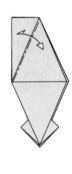

20. Precrease with a mountain fold.

21. Unfold.

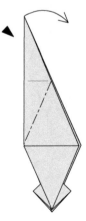

22. Reverse fold.

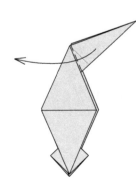

23. Valley fold over.

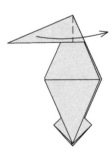

24. Valley fold again.

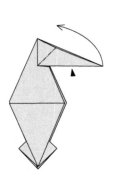

25. Squash fold.

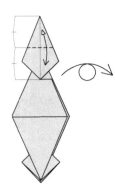

26. Precrease and turn over.

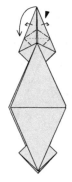

27. Squash fold, so as to make the top look the same on both sides.

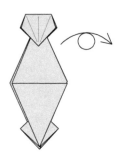

28. Turn over.

29. Precrease.

30. Precrease the top section in half.

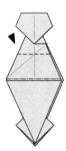

31. Reverse fold in and out. Note that the valley fold goes through the intersection of creases.

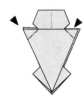

32. Reverse fold the thick corner at the left, and one corner at the right.

33. Tuck the flap into the pocket.

34. Mountain fold the corners in.

35. Open out the base. You can either crease sharply, or leave it rounded.

36. Completed **Pawn**.

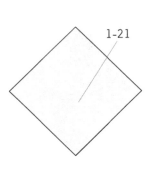

37. Begin with a same sized square for the Castle. Repeat steps 1-21.

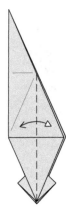

38. Precrease lightly. Repeat behind.

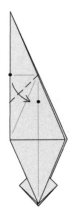

39. Valley fold, such that the dotted creases meet.

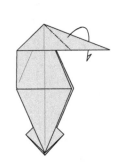

40. Mountain fold.

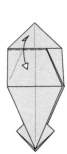

41. Precrease with a mountain fold.

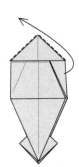

42. Open out the flap.

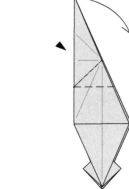

43. Squash fold.

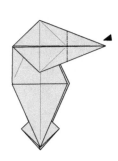

44. Sink the tip.

45. Valley fold the corners to the center.

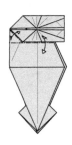

46. Precrease with mountain folds.

47. Open out.

48. Swing up.

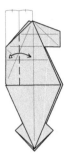

49. Precrease.

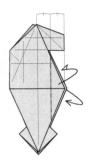

50. Mountain fold the sides in halfway.

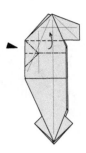

51. Crimp upwards, while pushing in the side.

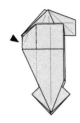

52. Sink halfway. Part of the sink is hidden.

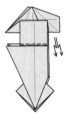

53. Form a very tiny crimp fold.

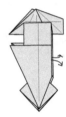

54. Pull out a layer from each side, allowing the upper edge to taper.

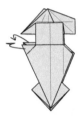

55. Mountain fold the two corners to match the right side.

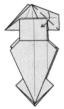

56. Valley fold over at each side to lock.

57. Open out the sides at a 90° angle.

58. View from above. Valley fold each corner up at a 90° angle.

59. Repeat steps 34-35.

60. Completed **Castle.**

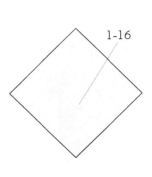

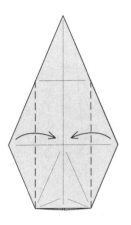

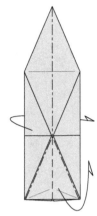

61. Begin with a same sized square for the Knight. Repeat steps 1-16.

62. Precrease.

63. Valley fold to the center. Do not crease sharply.

64. Mountain fold in half, while incorporating a reverse fold.

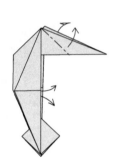

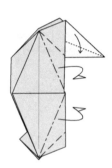

65. Reverse fold the center layer through.

66. Reverse fold.

67. Pull out a layer from each side. Do not completely flatten.

68. Swivel fold in all of the sides and flatten.

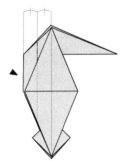

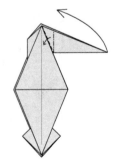

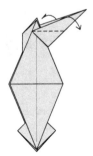

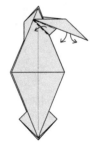

69. Closed sink the center flap halfway.

70. Crimp fold upwards.

71. Outside reverse fold.

72. Pull out a single layer from each side as far as possible.

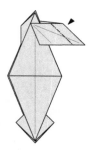

73. Closed reverse fold.

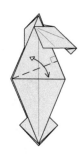

74. Outside reverse fold.

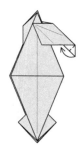

75. Precrease.

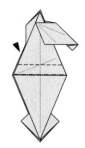

76. Reverse fold in and out. Note that the valley fold goes through the intersection of creases.

77. Repeat steps 32-36.

78. Completed **Knight**.

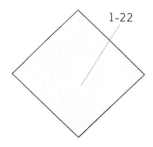

79. Begin with a same sized square for the Bishop. Repeat steps 1-22.

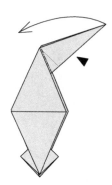

80. Reverse fold.

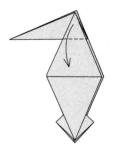

81. Open out.

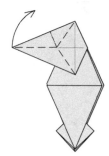

82. Rabbit ear.

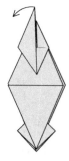

83. Undo the rabbit-ear.

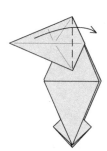

84. Swing the flap over.

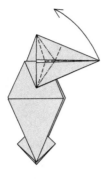

85. Redo the rabbit-ear, while adding additional folds.

86. Swing back.

87. Outside reverse fold.

88. Pull out a single layer at each side.

89. Precrease.

90. Valley fold to the intersection of creases.

91. Valley fold to the center.

92. Unfold.

93. Closed reverse fold.

94. Valley fold down at each side.

95. Reverse fold.

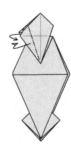

96. Mountain fold at each side.

97. Valley fold up.

98. Reverse fold.

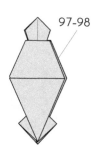

99. Repeat steps 97-98 behind.

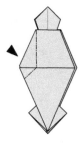

100. Invert the corner. The model will not lie flat.

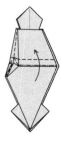

101. Crimp fold both sides to flatten.

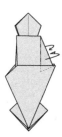

102. Swivel fold in both sides.

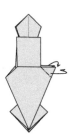

103. Mountain fold the two corners.

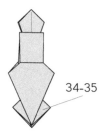

104. Repeat steps 34-35.

105. Completed **Bishop.**

106. Begin with a same sized square for the Queen. Repeat steps 1-22.

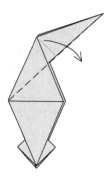

107. Swing down lightly.

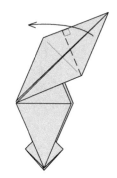

108. Valley fold over.

109. Valley fold up.

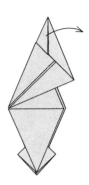

110. Unfold the pleat.

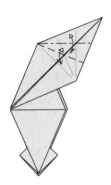

111. Repeat the precreases from steps 108 and 109 in the opposite direction.

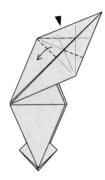

112. Squash fold.

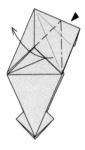

113. Squash fold again.

114. Pull out a single layer.

115. Squash fold.

116. Valley fold up.

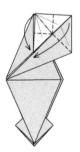

117. Swing the flap down, while incorporating a reverse fold.

118. Reverse fold twice.

119. Swing the center flap over.

120. Flip the cluster of flaps upwards.

121. Swing up.

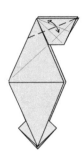

122. Precrease.

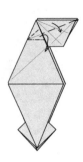

123. Swivel fold.

124. Repeat steps 122-123 behind.

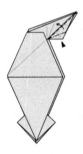

125. Spread squash.

126. Mountain fold.

127. Reverse fold one layer through.

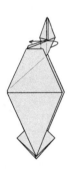

128. Valley fold, so as to align along the center.

129. Turn over.

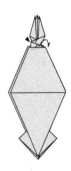

130. Swivel fold the double layer.

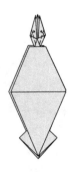

131. Valley fold the top layers to the center.

132. Turn over.

133. Valley fold to the center.

134. Pull out the side flaps.

135. Repeat steps 100-104.

136. Completed **Queen**.

137. Begin with a same sized square for the King. Repeat steps 1-22.

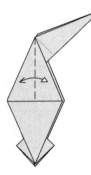

138. Precrease in half lightly.

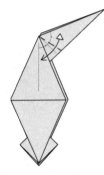

139. Bring the flap along the center and unfold.

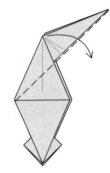

140. Lightly open out the flap.

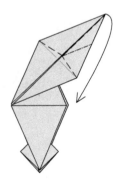

141. Rabbit ear using the existing creases.

142. Wrap around a single layer.

143. Swing over.

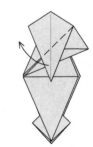

144. Valley fold up lightly.

145. Wrap around a single layer.

146. Swing down.

147. Pull the flap up while collapsing.

148. Precrease.

148-149

149. Valley fold, allowing the edges to meet the indicated intersections.

150. Repeat steps 148-149 behind.

151. Mountain fold the sides.

152. Precrease.

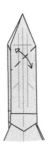

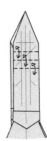

153. Closed sink the corner in and out.

154. Precrease into thirds.

155. Precrease.

156. Precrease using the intersection of creases as guides.

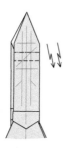

157. Crimp fold along the existing creases. The inner layers will not be symmetrical.

158. Valley fold over, pulling some paper from inside the crimp.

159. Swing through.

160. Swivel fold the sides inwards, allowing two reverse folds to form at the right. The flap will swing down.

161. Swing the flap up, tucking the excess into the pocket behind.

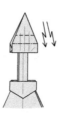

162. Crimp fold the tip.

163. Reverse fold the tip.

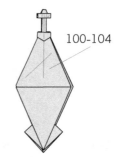

100-104

164. Repeat steps 100-104.

165. Completed **King**.

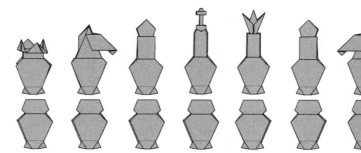

166. Completed *Chess Pieces*.

Chessboard

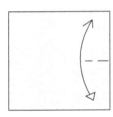

1. Pinch the edge in half.

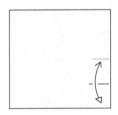

2. Pinch the lower section in half.

3. Valley fold the corner to the crease.

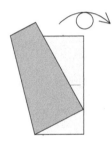

4. Turn over.

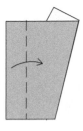

5. Valley fold to the intersection of raw edges.

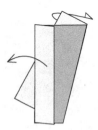

6. Unfold completely.

7. Precrease into fourths.

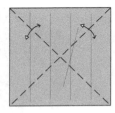

8. Precrease along the diagonals.

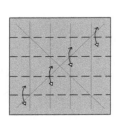

9. Precrease using the intersections of the diagonals as a guide.

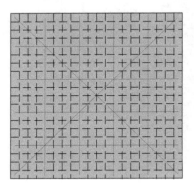

10. Divide each section further into fourths with valley folds.

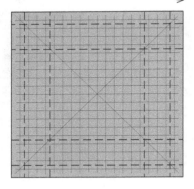

11. Add additional precreases (divide the 2nd and 5th columns and rows from the edges in half). Rotate the model.

1/8

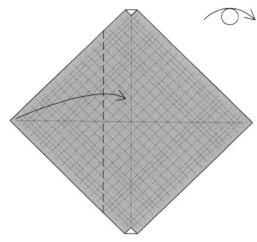

12. Valley fold the corners in (one unit).

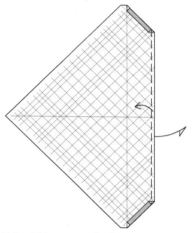

13. Valley fold inwards. This fold is touching the folds made in step 11. Turn over.

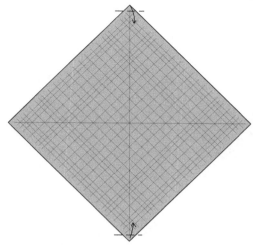

14. Valley fold the two edges to the nearest crease.

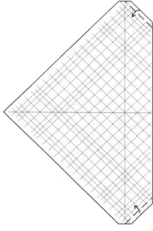

15. Valley fold, swinging the flap from behind to the forefront.

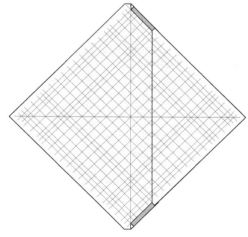

16. Turn over.

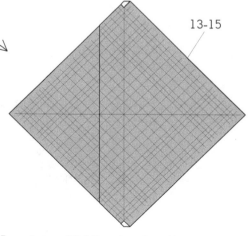

13-15

17. Repeat steps 13-15 on the other side.

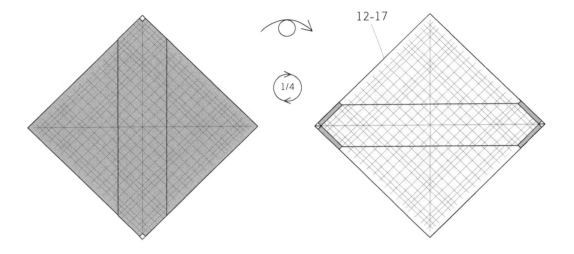

18. Turn over and rotate.

19. Repeat steps 12-17.

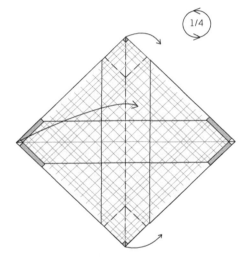

20. Valley fold in half while incorporating reverse folds. Rotate the model.

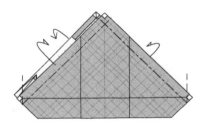

21. Swivel fold in the sides. The layers will overlap at the top corners.

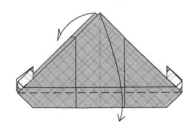

22. Valley fold down.

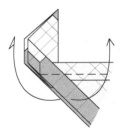

23. Valley fold up.

24. Valley fold the sides down.

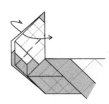

25. Wrap around the top point, reverse folding at the bottom corners. Repeat on the other side.

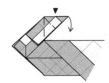

26. Squash fold. Repeat at the other side.

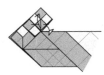

27. Flip the square. Repeat at the other side.

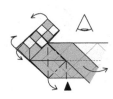

28. Spread squash the bottom, allowing the side flaps to swing outwards.

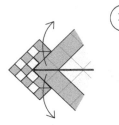

1/4

29. View from step 28. Spread apart the pleats. Rotate the model.

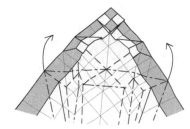

30. Reform, changing the direction of some of the folds. Form the horizontal mountain folds first. Repeat steps 29-30 at the bottom.

31. Pull out a single layer (you will have to raise the flap slightly to do this).

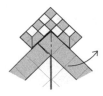

32. Open out the hem forming a squash fold at the top.

31-32

33. Repeat steps 31-32 on the remaining three hems.

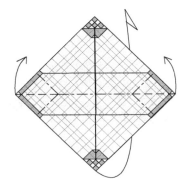

34. Mountain fold in half while incorporating reverse folds.

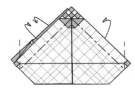

35. Swivel fold in the sides.

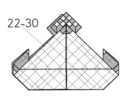

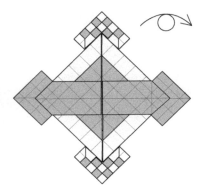

36. Repeat steps 22-30.

37. Valley fold outwards.

38. Turn over.

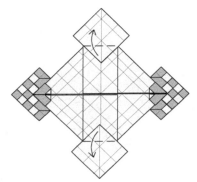

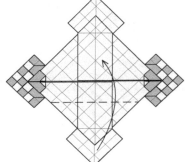

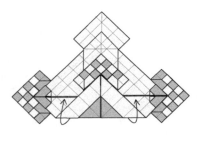

39. Valley fold outwards.

40. Valley fold up.

41. Wrap a single layer around at each side.

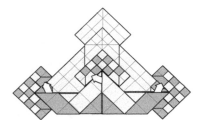

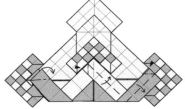

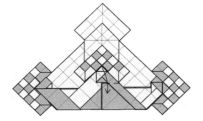

42. Pull out a single layer at the three indicated flaps.

43. At the left, reverse fold the corner back in (you will have to raise the flap slightly). On the other side, swivel fold the hem over, squash folding the corners.

44. Swing the flap down.

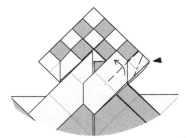

45. Spread squash the corner. The section will not lie flat.

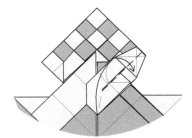

46. Close back up.

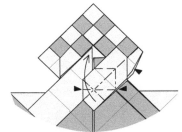

47. Closed sink the top corner while collapsing the bottom point and swinging it upwards.

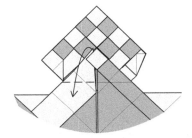

48. Swing the flap down.

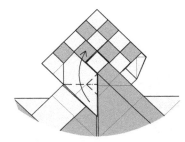

49. Valley fold back up while incorporating a reverse fold.

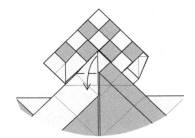

50. Valley fold down.

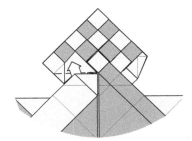

51. Unsink a single layer.

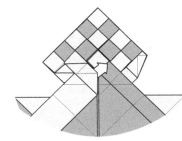

52. Open out slightly and release a single layer.

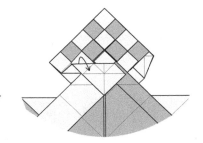

53. Wrap around a single layer.

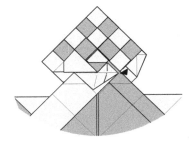

54. Reverse fold (you will have to raise the flap slightly to do this).

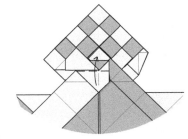

55. Swing the flap up.

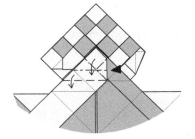

56. Collapse the flap downwards.

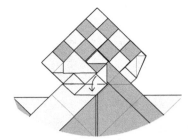

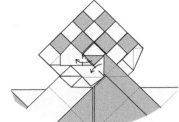

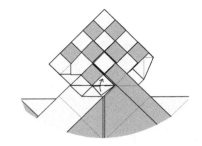

57. Swing the flap down lightly.

58. Swivel fold over.

59. Swing the flap back up.

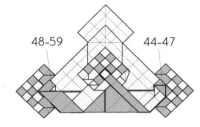

48-59   44-47

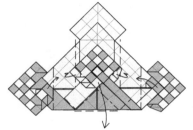

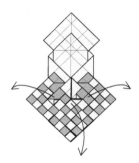

60. Repeat steps 48-59 at the left and steps 44-47 at the right.

61. Crimp the side squares inwards while collapsing the center square downwards. Allow the squares to interlock.

62. Open out, folding the center square out of the way.

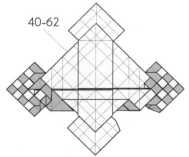

40-62

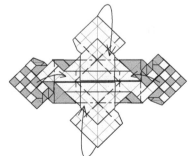

63. Repeat steps 40-62 at the top.

64. Collapse all of the squares inwards, using the folds from step 61. At 64 steps, this will work out to one step per square.

65. Completed *Chessboard*.

CPSIA information can be obtained
at www.ICGtesting.com
Printed in the USA
LVHW061322210720
661197LV00003B/16